Pasta

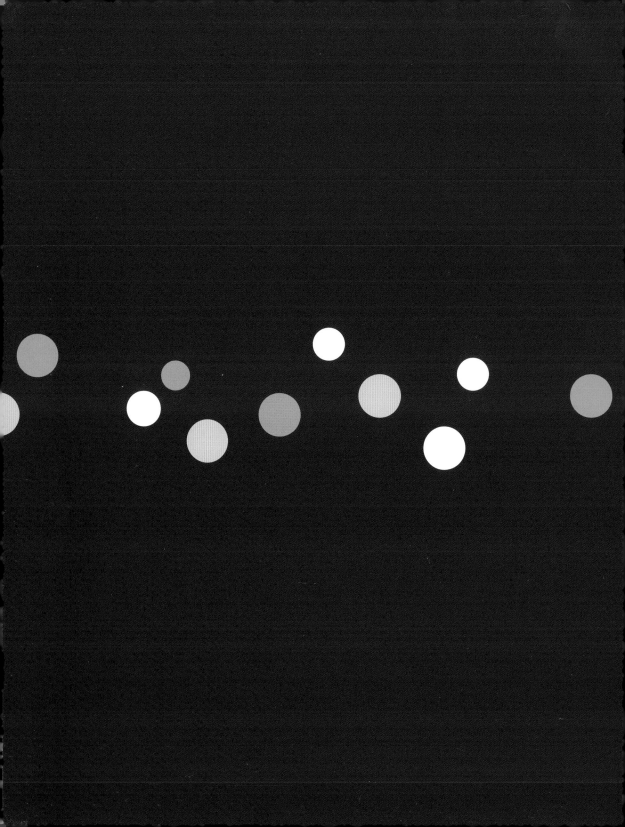

Pasta

Jane Price

MURDOCH BOOKS

contents

pasta pronto

It was famous film director Federico Fellini who said, 'Life is a combination of magic and pasta.' He obviously knew what he was talking about. It is not only the Italians who are passionate about their pasta—it has become a staple in kitchens all around the world.

It is difficult to go wrong with pasta. Even the simplest pasta recipe, such as butter and shavings of parmesan melted over some fresh tagliatelle, can be exquisite. All you have to remember is that pasta should be cooked until *al dente* which in Italian literally means 'to the tooth'.

Many people assume that fresh pasta is better than dried but it depends on the sauce. If you are using a rich sauce made from cream, butter and cheese, then fresh pasta is ideal. Dried pasta is the better alternative when you have a tomato-based sauce. Of course, these rules aren't set in stone. Part of the appeal of pasta is its versatility and variety, so be adventurous and experiment with different types, shapes and flavors.

There are a few simple guidelines that should be followed when cooking pasta to ensure the best results. Short pastas are best with meat and tomato sauces, as the tubes catch the sauce in their holes. Filled and flavored pasta should be paired with simple sauces. Long thin pasta go well with simple sauces, and the flatter types work well with creamy sauces that stick to their lengths. Curly shapes suit thick, chunky sauces which get caught in their shape. *Buon appetito!*

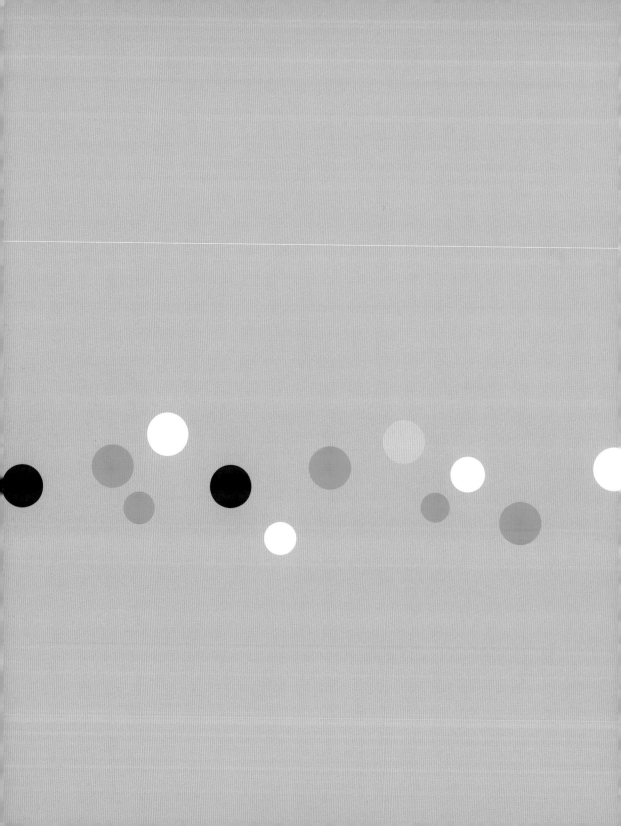

short

Penne all'arrabbiata

2 tablespoons olive oil
2 large garlic cloves, thinly sliced
1–2 dried chilies
1 lb 12 oz canned tomatoes
4½ cups penne
1 basil sprig, torn into pieces

Cook the pasta in a large saucepan of boiling salted water until *al dente*. Drain well and return to the pan to keep warm.

Meanwhile, heat the olive oil in a saucepan over low heat. Add the garlic and chilies and cook until the garlic is light golden brown. Turn the chilies over during cooking so both sides get a chance to infuse in the oil. Add the tomatoes and season with salt. Cook gently, breaking up the tomatoes with a wooden spoon, for 20–30 minutes, or until the sauce is rich and thick.

Add the basil to the sauce and toss with the pasta. Season to taste.

SERVES 4

Artichoke risoni

1 oz butter
1 tablespoon olive oil
2 fennel bulbs, sliced
1½ cups drained and chopped marinated
    artichoke hearts
10½ fl oz light whipping cream
1 tablespoon dijon mustard
3 tablespoons dry white wine
½ cup grated parmesan cheese
1½ cups risoni
2 cups shredded spinach
toasted Italian bread, to serve

Heat the butter and oil in a frying pan over medium heat. Add the fennel and cook for 20 minutes, or until caramelized. Add the artichoke and cook for a further 5–10 minutes.

Stir in the cream, mustard, white wine, and parmesan and bring to a boil. Reduce the heat and simmer for 5 minutes.

Meanwhile, cook the pasta in a large saucepan of boiling salted water until *al dente*. Drain well and return to the pan to keep warm.

Add the pasta and spinach to the sauce and cook until the spinach has wilted. Serve with toasted Italian bread.

SERVES 4

Orecchiette with baby spinach and squash

1 lb 10 oz winter squash, such as butternut or jap
2 tablespoons parmesan-infused olive oil (see Notes)
16 unpeeled garlic cloves
1²/₃ cups halved cherry tomatoes
4½ cups orecchiette
4 cups baby spinach leaves
1⅓ cups marinated Persian feta cheese (see Notes)
3 tablespoons sherry vinegar
2 tablespoons walnut oil

Preheat the oven to 400°F. Cut the squash into large cubes, put in a roasting tin and drizzle with the parmesan-infused oil. Roast for 30 minutes, then add the garlic. Arrange the tomatoes on a baking tray. Place all the vegetables in the oven and roast for 10–15 minutes, or until cooked. Don't overcook the tomatoes.

Meanwhile, cook the pasta in a large saucepan of boiling salted water until *al dente*. Drain well and return to the pan to keep warm.

Toss together the pasta, tomatoes, squash, garlic, and spinach in a large bowl. Drain the feta, reserving 3 tablespoons of marinade. Whisk the reserved marinade, sherry vinegar, and walnut oil together. Pour over the pasta and sprinkle with pieces of the feta.

SERVES 4

NOTES: Parmesan-infused olive oil is available at gourmet food stores and adds depth of flavor. Persian feta is softer and creamier than other feta and is marinated in oil, herbs, and garlic.

Creamy pesto
chicken penne

1 tablespoon oil
1½ oz butter
2 small boneless, skinless
   chicken breasts
8 thin, fresh asparagus, cut into
   1½-inch lengths
3 scallions, chopped
4 garlic cloves, crushed
1¼ cups sour cream
½ cup light whipping cream

¾ cup chicken stock
1 cup grated parmesan cheese
½ cup finely chopped basil
2 tablespoons toasted pine nuts
4½ cups penne
basil leaves, to garnish

Heat the oil and half the butter in a large frying pan over high heat. Add the chicken and cook for 5 minutes on each side, or until just cooked. Remove, cover and cool, then cut into ½-inch thick slices.

Add the asparagus and scallions to the pan and cook for 2 minutes, or until the asparagus is just tender. Remove. Wipe the pan with paper towel.

Reduce the heat to medium and add the remaining butter and the garlic. Cook for 2 minutes, or until light golden brown. Add the sour cream, cream, and stock, and simmer for 10 minutes or until reduced slightly. Add the parmesan and basil and stir for 2 minutes, or until the cheese has melted. Return the chicken and asparagus to the pan. Add the pine nuts and cook for 2 minutes to heat through. Season.

Meanwhile, cook the pasta in a large saucepan of boiling salted water until *al dente*. Drain well and return to the pan to keep warm.

Combine the sauce and the pasta. Garnish with basil leaves.

SERVES 4

Pasta gnocchi with broiled peppers

6 large red peppers, halved
14 oz pasta gnocchi (see Note)
2 tablespoons olive oil
1 onion, thinly sliced
3 garlic cloves, finely chopped
2 tablespoons shredded basil
whole basil leaves, to garnish
shaved parmesan cheese, to serve

Cut the peppers into large flattish pieces. Cook, skin side up, under a hot broiler until the skin blackens and blisters. Cool in a plastic bag, then peel the skin.

Cook the pasta in a large saucepan of boiling salted water until *al dente*. Drain well and return to the pan to keep warm.

Meanwhile, heat the oil in a large frying pan, add the onion and garlic and cook over medium heat for 5 minutes, or until soft. Slice 1 pepper into thin strips and add to the onion mixture.

Chop the remaining pepper, then purée in a food processor until smooth. Add to the onion mixture and cook over low heat for 5 minutes, or until warmed through.

Toss together the sauce and pasta. Season, then stir in the shredded basil. Garnish with the basil leaves and serve with the parmesan.

SERVES 4–6

NOTE: Pasta gnocchi is similar in shape to potato gnocchi. If unavailable, use conchiglie or orecchiette.

Penne with mushroom and herb sauce

2 tablespoons olive oil
4½ cups sliced button mushrooms
2 garlic cloves, crushed
2 teaspoons chopped marjoram
½ cup dry white wine
4 tablespoons light whipping cream
4 cups penne
1 tablespoon lemon juice
1 teaspoon finely grated lemon zest
2 tablespoons chopped Italian parsley
½ cup grated parmesan cheese

Heat the oil in a large heavy-based frying pan over high heat. Add the mushrooms and cook for 3 minutes, stirring constantly to prevent the mushrooms from burning. Add the garlic and marjoram and cook for a further 2 minutes.

Add the white wine to the pan, reduce the heat and simmer for 5 minutes or until nearly all the liquid has evaporated. Stir in the cream and cook over low heat for 5 minutes, or until the sauce has thickened.

Meanwhile, cook the pasta in a large saucepan of boiling salted water until *al dente*. Drain well and return to the pan to keep warm.

Add the lemon juice, zest, parsley, and half the parmesan to the sauce. Season to taste. Toss the pasta through the sauce and sprinkle with the remaining parmesan.

SERVES 4

Casarecce with roasted tomatoes, arugula, and goat's cheese

16 plum tomatoes
1 handful basil leaves, torn
3¼ cups casarecce
4 tablespoons olive oil
2 garlic cloves, finely sliced
2 tablespoons lemon juice
2⅔ cups roughly chopped arugula
2 tablespoons chopped Italian parsley
4 tablespoons grated parmesan cheese
3¾ cups crumbled goat's cheese

Preheat the oven to 325°F. Score a cross in the base of the tomatoes. Put in a heatproof bowl, and cover with boiling water. Leave for about 30 seconds, then transfer to cold water and peel the skin away from the cross. Cut in half and place cut-side up on a wire rack over a baking tray. Season liberally and scatter with the basil leaves. Put the tray in the oven and bake for about 3 hours.

Meanwhile, cook the pasta in a large saucepan of boiling salted water until *al dente*. Drain well and return to the pan to keep warm.

Heat the olive oil and garlic over low–medium heat until it just begins to sizzle. Remove immediately and add to the pasta with the tomatoes, lemon juice, arugula, parsley, and parmesan. Stir gently to combine, allowing the heat from the pasta to wilt the arugula. Serve topped with the crumbled goat's cheese.

SERVES 4

Macaroni cheese
with pancetta

2½ cups macaroni
2½ oz piece pancetta, diced
2 cups light whipping cream
1 cup grated cheddar cheese
2 cups grated gruyère cheese
1 cup grated parmesan cheese
1 garlic clove, crushed
2 teaspoons dijon mustard
½ teaspoon paprika
2 tablespoons snipped chives, plus extra to garnish

Cook the pasta in a large saucepan of boiling salted water until *al dente*. Drain well and return to the pan to keep warm.

Meanwhile, cook the pancetta in a large saucepan over high heat, stirring, for 4 minutes or until well browned and slightly crisp. Drain on paper towel. Reduce the heat to medium, stir in the cream and simmer. Add the cheeses, garlic, mustard, and paprika. Stir for 5 minutes, or until the cheeses have melted and the sauce has thickened. Season.

Add the pasta and pancetta and stir for 1 minute, or until heated through. Stir in the chives, garnish with the extra chives and serve.

SERVES 4

Penne with pork and fennel sausages

6 Italian pork and fennel sausages (about 1 lb 4 oz)
1 tablespoon olive oil
1 small red onion, finely chopped
2–3 garlic cloves, crushed
½ teaspoon chili flakes
4½ cups thinly sliced field or button mushrooms
1 lb 12 oz canned chopped tomatoes
1 tablespoon finely chopped thyme
5½ cups penne rigate
grated parmesan cheese, to serve

Split the sausages open, remove and crumble the filling and discard the skins.

Heat the oil in a large saucepan over medium–high heat. Cook the onion for
3–4 minutes, or until fragrant and transparent. Add the garlic, chili flakes,
mushrooms, and crumbled sausage meat. Cook over high heat, stirring gently to
mash the sausage meat, for 4–5 minutes, or until the meat is evenly browned.
Continue to cook, stirring once or twice, for about 10 minutes.

Stir in the tomato and thyme, then bring the sauce to a boil. Cover and cook
over medium–low heat for 20 minutes, stirring occasionally to make sure the sauce
doesn't stick to the bottom of the pan.

Meanwhile, cook the pasta in a large saucepan of boiling salted water until *al dente*.
Drain well and return to the pan to keep warm.

Add the pasta to the sauce and stir to combine. Serve with the parmesan.

SERVES 4

Orecchiette
with broccoli

2 whole broccoli, cut into florets
4 cups orecchiette
3 tablespoons extra virgin olive oil
½ teaspoon dried chili flakes
4 tablespoons grated pecorino or parmesan cheese

Blanch the broccoli in a large saucepan of boiling salted water for 5 minutes, or until just tender. Remove with a slotted spoon, drain well and return the water to the boil.

Cook the pasta in the boiling water until *al dente*. Drain well and return to the pan to keep warm.

Meanwhile, heat the oil in a heavy-based frying pan over medium heat. Add the chili flakes and broccoli and cook, stirring, for 5 minutes, or until the broccoli is well coated and beginning to break apart. Season. Add to the pasta, stir through the cheese and serve.

SERVES 6

Eggplant, ricotta, and pasta pots

1⅓ cups straight macaroni
½ cup olive oil
1 large eggplant, cut lengthways into ½-inch thick slices
1 small onion, finely chopped
2 garlic cloves, crushed
14 oz canned chopped tomatoes

1⅔ cups ricotta cheese
1 cup coarsely grated parmesan cheese
3 tablespoons shredded basil, plus extra to garnish

Preheat the oven to 350°F. Cook the pasta in a large saucepan of boiling salted water until *al dente*. Drain well and return to the pan to keep warm.

Heat 2 tablespoons of the oil in a non-stick frying pan over medium heat. Cook the eggplant in three batches for 2–3 minutes on each side, or until golden, adding 2 tablespoons of oil with each batch. Remove and drain well on paper towel.

Add the onion and garlic to the pan and cook over medium heat for 2–3 minutes, or until just golden. Add the tomato and cook for 5 minutes, or until most of the liquid has evaporated. Season.

Combine the ricotta, parmesan, basil, and pasta in a bowl. Line the base and sides of four 1½-cup ramekins with eggplant, trimming any overhanging pieces. Top with half the pasta mix, pressing down firmly. Spoon over the tomato sauce, then cover with the remaining pasta mixture. Bake for 10–15 minutes, or until heated through. Stand for 5 minutes, then run a knife around the ramekin to loosen. Invert onto plates and garnish with basil.

SERVES 4

Casarecce with squash and feta

2 lbs 4 oz winter squash, such as butternut,
    peeled and cut into ¾-inch chunks
1 red onion, thinly sliced
8 garlic cloves, unpeeled
1 tablespoon rosemary leaves
4 tablespoons olive oil
3¼ cups casarecce
1⅓ cups crumbled marinated feta cheese
2 tablespoons grated parmesan cheese
2 tablespoons finely chopped Italian parsley

Preheat the oven to 400°F. Put the squash, onion, garlic, and rosemary in a roasting tin. Drizzle with 1 tablespoon of the oil and season. Rub the oil over all the vegetables and herbs until well coated. Roast for 30 minutes, or until the squash is soft and starting to caramelize.

Cook the pasta in a large saucepan of boiling salted water until *al dente*. Drain well and return to the pan to keep warm.

Squeeze the roasted garlic out of its skin and place it in a bowl with the remaining oil. Mash with a fork.

Add the garlic oil to the pasta, then stir through the remaining ingredients. Toss to combine. Season to taste.

SERVES 4

Penne carbonara

4½ cups penne
1 tablespoon olive oil
7 oz piece pancetta or bacon, cut into long thin strips
6 egg yolks
¾ cup light whipping cream
¾ cup grated parmesan cheese

Cook the pasta in a large saucepan of boiling salted water until *al dente*. Drain well and return to the pan to keep warm.

Meanwhile, heat the oil in a frying pan over high heat. Cook the pancetta for 6 minutes, or until crisp and golden. Remove with a slotted spoon and drain on paper towel.

Beat the egg yolks, cream, and parmesan together in a bowl and season well.

Return the pasta to its saucepan and pour the egg mixture over the pasta, tossing gently. Add the pancetta and cook over very low heat for 30–60 seconds, or until the sauce thickens and coats the pasta. Season and serve immediately.

SERVES 4–6

NOTE: Be careful not to cook the pasta over high heat once you have added the egg mixture, or the sauce risks being scrambled by the heat.

Orecchiette with cauliflower, bacon, and pecorino

1 lb 10 oz cauliflower, cut into florets
4 cups orecchiette (see Note)
½ cup olive oil, plus extra, to drizzle
3 bacon slices, diced
2 garlic cloves, finely chopped
½ cup pine nuts, toasted
½ cup grated pecorino cheese
½ cup chopped Italian parsley
¾ cup fresh breadcrumbs, toasted

Bring a large saucepan of salted water to a boil and cook the cauliflower for 5–6 minutes, or until tender. Drain.

Cook the pasta in a large saucepan of boiling salted water until *al dente*. Drain well and return to the pan to keep warm.

Heat the oil in a frying pan over medium heat. Cook the bacon for 4–5 minutes, or until just crisp. Add the garlic and cook for 1 minute, or until just golden. Add the cauliflower and toss well.

Add the pasta to the pan with the pine nuts, pecorino cheese, parsley, and ½ cup of the breadcrumbs and stir to combine. Season, sprinkle with the remaining breadcrumbs and drizzle with a little extra oil.

SERVES 4

NOTE: Orecchiette means 'little ears' in Italian. If unavailable, use conchiglie or cavatelli.

Zucchini pasta bake

1 cup risoni
1½ oz butter
4 scallions, thinly sliced
3 cups grated zucchini
4 eggs
½ cup light whipping cream
4 tablespoons ricotta cheese (see Note)
⅔ cup grated mozzarella cheese
¾ cup grated parmesan cheese

Preheat the oven to 350°F. Cook the pasta in a large saucepan of boiling salted water until *al dente*. Drain well and return to the pan to keep warm.

Meanwhile, heat the butter in a frying pan over medium heat. Add the scallions and cook for 1 minute. Add the zucchini and cook for a further 4 minutes, or until soft. Allow to cool slightly.

Combine the eggs, cream, ricotta, mozzarella, pasta, and half of the parmesan. Stir in the zucchini mixture. Season well. Spoon into four 2-cup greased ovenproof dishes. Sprinkle with the remaining parmesan and bake for 25–30 minutes, or until firm and golden.

SERVES 4

NOTE: With such simple flavors, it is important to use good-quality fresh ricotta from the delicatessen or the deli section of your local supermarket.

Penne with tomato and basil sauce

5½ cups penne rigate
4 tablespoons extra virgin olive oil
4 garlic cloves, crushed
4 anchovy fillets, finely chopped
2 small red chilies, seeded and finely chopped
6 large vine-ripened tomatoes, peeled, seeded and diced
4 tablespoons white wine
1 tablespoon concentrated tomato purée
2 teaspoons sugar
2 tablespoons finely chopped Italian parsley
3 tablespoons shredded basil
grated parmesan cheese, to serve (optional)

Cook the pasta in a large saucepan of boiling salted water until *al dente*. Drain well and return to the pan to keep warm.

Meanwhile, heat the oil in a frying pan over medium heat. Cook the garlic for 30 seconds. Stir in the anchovy and chili and cook for a further 30 seconds. Increase the heat to high, add the tomato and cook for 2 minutes. Add the wine, tomato purée and sugar and simmer, covered, for 10 minutes, or until thickened.

Toss the tomato sauce and herbs through the pasta. Season and serve with grated parmesan, if desired.

SERVES 4

Conchiglie with spring vegetables

6 cups conchiglie rigate
2 cups frozen peas
2 cups frozen fava beans, blanched and peeled
4 tablespoons olive oil
6 scallions, cut into 1¼-inch pieces
2 garlic cloves, finely chopped
1 cup vegetable or chicken stock
12 thin, fresh asparagus spears, cut into 2-inch lengths
½ teaspoon finely grated lemon zest
3 tablespoons lemon juice
shaved parmesan cheese, to garnish

Cook the pasta in a large saucepan of boiling salted water until *al dente*. Drain well and return to the pan to keep warm.

Meanwhile, put the peas in a saucepan of boiling water and cook over high heat for 1–2 minutes, or until tender. Remove with a slotted spoon and plunge into cold water. Add the fava beans to the saucepan of boiling water and cook for 1–2 minutes, then drain and plunge into cold water. Remove and slip the skins off.

Heat 2 tablespoons of the oil in a frying pan over medium heat. Add the scallions and garlic and cook for 2 minutes, or until softened. Pour in the stock and cook for 5 minutes, or until slightly reduced. Add the asparagus and cook for 3–4 minutes, or until bright green and just tender. Stir in the peas and fava beans and cook for 2–3 minutes, or until heated through.

Toss the remaining oil through the pasta, then add the vegetables, lemon zest, and lemon juice. Season and toss together well. Serve topped with shaved parmesan.

SERVES 4

Orecchiette with mushrooms, pancetta, and smoked mozzarella

3½ cups orecchiette
2 tablespoons olive oil
5½ oz piece pancetta, cut into short thin strips
2¼ cups sliced button mushrooms
2 leeks, sliced
1 cup light whipping cream
1⅓ cups smoked mozzarella, cut into ½-inch cubes
8 basil leaves, torn

Cook the pasta in a large saucepan of boiling salted water until *al dente*. Drain well and return to the pan to keep warm.

Meanwhile, heat the oil in a large frying pan over medium–high heat. Add the pancetta, mushrooms, and leek and sauté for 5 minutes. Stir in the cream and season with pepper. Simmer over low heat for 5 minutes. Stir in the pasta. Add the mozzarella and basil and toss.

SERVES 4

Penne with roasted tomato and pesto

4¾ fl oz olive oil
3⅓ cups cherry tomatoes
5 garlic cloves, unpeeled
4½ cups penne
4 tablespoons pesto
3 tablespoons balsamic vinegar
basil leaves, to garnish

Preheat the oven to 350°F. Put 2 tablespoons of oil in a roasting dish and place in the oven for 5 minutes. Add the tomatoes and garlic to the dish, season well and toss until the tomatoes are well coated. Return to the oven and roast for 30 minutes.

Meanwhile, cook the pasta in a large saucepan of boiling salted water until *al dente*. Drain well and return to the pan to keep warm.

Squeeze the flesh from the roasted garlic cloves into a bowl. Add the remaining olive oil, the pesto, vinegar, and 3 tablespoons of the tomato cooking juices. Season and toss to combine. Add to the pasta and mix well. Gently stir in the cherry tomatoes, then scatter with basil.

SERVES 4

Farfalle with spinach and bacon

4½ cups farfalle
2 tablespoons extra virgin olive oil
4 bacon slices, chopped
1 red onion, finely chopped
5 cups baby spinach leaves
1–2 tablespoons sweet chili sauce (optional)
3 tablespoons crumbled goat's cheese

Cook the pasta in a large saucepan of boiling salted water until *al dente*. Drain well and return to the pan to keep warm.

Meanwhile, heat the oil in a frying pan over medium heat. Add the bacon and cook for 3 minutes, or until golden. Add the onion and cook for a further 4 minutes, or until softened. Toss the spinach leaves through the onion and bacon mixture for 30 seconds, or until just wilted.

Add the bacon and spinach mixture to the pasta, then stir in the sweet chili sauce, if using. Season and toss well. Scatter with the crumbled goat's cheese to serve.

SERVES 4

Penne with tomato and onion jam and olives

3 tablespoons olive oil
4 red onions, sliced
1 tablespoon brown sugar
2 tablespoons balsamic vinegar
1 lb 12 oz canned chopped tomatoes
5½ cups penne rigate
1 cup small pitted black olives
¾ cup grated parmesan cheese

Heat the oil in a non-stick frying pan over medium heat. Add the onion and sugar and cook for 25–30 minutes, or until caramelized.

Stir in the vinegar, bring to a boil and cook for 5 minutes. Add the tomatoes, return to a boil, then reduce the heat to medium–low and simmer for about 25 minutes, or until the tomatoes are reduced and jam-like.

Meanwhile, cook the pasta in a large saucepan of boiling salted water until *al dente*. Drain well and return to the pan to keep warm. Add the tomato mixture and olives and stir to combine. Season and top with the grated parmesan.

SERVES 4

Porcini mushroom and walnut penne

¾ oz porcini mushrooms
4½ cups penne
2 tablespoons olive oil
1 onion, finely chopped
2 garlic cloves, crushed
8 oz button mushrooms (about 24), sliced
3 thyme sprigs
¾ cup walnuts
2 tablespoons sour cream
grated parmesan cheese, to serve

Put the porcini in a bowl with just enough boiling water to cover and leave to soak for 30 minutes. If they soak up all the water quickly, add a little more.

Cook the pasta in a large saucepan of boiling salted water until *al dente*. Drain well and return to the pan to keep warm.

Heat the oil in a deep frying pan over medium heat. Add the onion and garlic and cook until translucent but not browned. Add the porcini and any soaking liquid, mushrooms, and thyme. The mushrooms will give off liquid as they cook so continue cooking until the liquid is soaked up again.

In a separate frying pan, fry the walnuts over medium heat without any oil until they start to brown and smell toasted. Allow to cool slightly, then roughly chop and add to the mushroom mixture. Toss with the pasta, stir through the sour cream and season. Serve with the parmesan.

SERVES 4

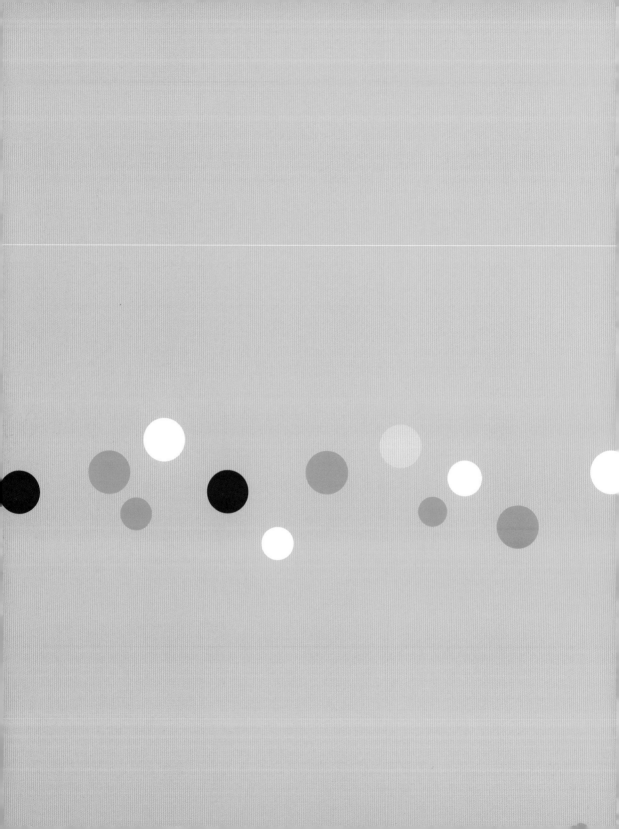

filled

Conchiglione stuffed with roast squash and ricotta

2 lbs 4 oz winter squash, such as butternut,
    cut into large wedges
olive oil, to drizzle
10 unpeeled garlic cloves
2 cups ricotta cheese
1/3 cup finely shredded basil
3 cups bottled pasta sauce
1/2 cup dry white wine
56 conchiglione or 32 giant conchiglione
1 cup grated parmesan cheese

Preheat the oven to 400°F. Place the squash in a baking dish, drizzle with olive oil and season. Bake for 30 minutes, then add the garlic and bake for 15 minutes or until tender. Allow to cool slightly, then peel and mash the squash and garlic. Mix with the ricotta and half the basil and season to taste.

Put the pasta sauce and wine in a saucepan and bring to a boil over medium heat. Reduce the heat and simmer for 10 minutes, or until slightly thickened.

Meanwhile, cook the pasta in a large saucepan of boiling salted water until *al dente*. Drain well. Lay out on a dish towel to dry, then fill with the squash mixture. Spread any remaining filling in a large ovenproof dish, top with the shells and pour on the sauce. Sprinkle with parmesan and the remaining basil and bake for about 15–20 minutes (or 30 minutes for the giant shells).

SERVES 6

Spinach and
ricotta ravioli

1 tablespoon olive oil
1 red onion, finely chopped
1 garlic clove, crushed
4 cups baby spinach leaves,
    coarsely chopped
1 cup ricotta cheese
2 egg yolks, beaten

2 tablespoons grated
    parmesan cheese
freshly grated nutmeg
48 won ton wrappers
1½ oz butter
2 tablespoons sage leaves

Heat the oil in a frying pan over low heat. Add the onion and garlic and fry for 2–3 minutes, or until the onion is soft and translucent. Add the spinach and stir until wilted.

Stir the spinach mixture into the ricotta, along with the egg yolk, parmesan, and some nutmeg. Season.

Brush a little water around the edge of a won ton wrapper and put 1 teaspoon of filling in the center. Fold the wrapper over to make a half moon shape and press the edges firmly together. Lay out the ravioli on a dish towel and repeat with the remaining wrappers.

Cook the pasta in a large saucepan of boiling salted water until *al dente*. Remove with a slotted spoon and drain well.

Melt the butter in a small saucepan over medium heat. Add the sage and cook for 1–2 minutes, or until the butter browns slightly. Pour the butter and sage mixture over the pasta and serve.

SERVES 4

Tortellini boscaiola

1 oz butter
4 bacon slices, chopped
2 garlic cloves, crushed
1 small leek, thinly sliced
10½ ounces brown or button mushrooms, sliced
3 tablespoons dry white wine
1½ cups light whipping cream
1 teaspoon chopped thyme
1 lb 2 oz fresh veal tortellini
½ cup grated parmesan cheese
1 tablespoon chopped Italian parsley

Melt the butter in a large frying pan over medium heat. Add the bacon and cook for 5 minutes, or until crisp. Add the garlic and leek, and cook for 2 minutes. Add the mushrooms and cook for 8 minutes, or until softened. Add the wine, cream, and thyme and bring to a boil. Reduce the heat and simmer for 10 minutes, or until the sauce has thickened.

Meanwhile, cook the pasta in a large saucepan of boiling salted water until *al dente*. Drain well and return to the pan to keep warm.

Add the parmesan to the sauce and stir over low heat until melted. Season. Combine the sauce with the pasta and parsley.

SERVES 4–6

Veal agnolotti with alfredo sauce

1 lb 6 oz veal agnolotti
3¼ oz butter
1½ cups grated parmesan cheese
10½ fl oz light whipping cream
2 tablespoons chopped marjoram (see Note)

Cook the pasta in a large saucepan of boiling salted water until *al dente*. Drain well and return to the pan to keep warm.

Meanwhile, melt the butter in a saucepan over low heat. Add the parmesan and cream and bring to a boil. Reduce the heat and simmer, stirring constantly, for 2 minutes, or until the sauce has thickened slightly. Stir in the marjoram and season. Toss the sauce through the pasta.

SERVES 4–6

NOTE: Any fresh herb such as parsley, thyme, chervil, or dill can be used instead of marjoram.

Ham and cheese pasta bake

1½ tablespoons olive oil
1 onion, finely chopped
10 thin slices ham, cut into 2-inch lengths
21 fl oz light whipping cream
10½ oz cooked fresh peas or frozen peas, thawed
13 oz conchiglione
3 tablespoons roughly chopped basil
2 cups grated sharp cheddar cheese

Preheat the oven to 400°F. Grease a 10-cup ovenproof ceramic dish.

Heat 1 tablespoon of the oil in a frying pan over medium heat. Cook the onion, stirring frequently, for 5 minutes, or until soft. Add the remaining oil, then the ham and cook, stirring, for 1 minute. Pour the cream into the pan, bring to a boil, then reduce the heat and simmer for 6 minutes. Add the peas and cook for a further 2–4 minutes, or until the mixture has thickened slightly. Season.

Meanwhile, cook the pasta in a large saucepan of boiling salted water until *al dente*. Drain well and return to the pan to keep warm.

Add the sauce to the pasta, then stir in the basil and three-quarters of the cheese. Season. Add the mixture to the prepared dish, sprinkle on the remaining cheese and bake for 20 minutes, or until the top is golden brown.

SERVES 4

Veal tortellini with creamy mushroom sauce

1 lb 2 oz veal tortellini
3 tablespoons olive oil
1 lb 5 oz brown mushrooms, thinly sliced
2 garlic cloves, crushed
½ cup dry white wine
10½ fl oz heavy whipping cream
pinch of ground nutmeg
3 tablespoons finely chopped Italian parsley
¼ cup grated parmesan cheese

Cook the pasta in a large saucepan of boiling salted water until *al dente*. Drain well and return to the pan to keep warm.

Meanwhile, heat the oil in a frying pan over medium heat. Add the mushrooms and cook, stirring occasionally, for 5 minutes, or until softened. Add the garlic and cook for 1 minute. Stir in the wine and cook for 5 minutes, or until the liquid has reduced by half.

Combine the cream, nutmeg, and parsley. Add to the sauce and cook for 3–5 minutes, or until the sauce thickens slightly. Season. Divide the tortellini among four serving plates and spoon over the mushroom sauce. Sprinkle with parmesan.

SERVES 4

Beet ravioli with sage burnt butter sauce

12 oz canned baby beets
1/3 cup grated parmesan cheese
1 cup fresh ricotta cheese
4 fresh lasagne sheets
fine cornmeal, for sprinkling
7 oz butter, chopped

40 sage leaves (about
    1/8 oz), torn
2 garlic cloves, crushed
shaved parmesan cheese,
    to serve

Drain the beets, then grate them into a bowl. Add the parmesan and ricotta and mix well. Lay a sheet of pasta on a flat surface and place evenly spaced tablespoons of the ricotta mixture on the pasta to give 12 mounds—four across and three down. Flatten the mounds of filling slightly. Lightly brush the edges of the pasta sheet and around each pile of filling with water.

Place a second sheet of pasta over the top and press around each mound to seal and enclose the filling. Using a pasta wheel or sharp knife, cut the pasta into 12 ravioli. Lay them out on a lined baking tray that has been sprinkled with cornmeal. Repeat with the remaining filling and lasagne sheets to make 24 ravioli. Gently remove any air bubbles after cutting so that they are completely sealed.

Cook the pasta in a large saucepan of boiling salted water until *al dente*. Drain well, then divide among four serving plates.

Meanwhile, melt the butter in a saucepan until golden brown. Remove from the heat, stir in the sage and garlic and spoon over the ravioli. Sprinkle with shaved parmesan and season.

SERVES 4

Roasted vegetable cannelloni

2¼ oz butter
1 large leek, cut into ½-inch thick pieces
7 oz chargrilled eggplant in oil
7 oz chargrilled sweet potato in oil
1 cup grated cheddar cheese
4 tablespoons all-purpose flour
4 cups milk
6 fresh lasagne sheets

Preheat the oven to 400°F. Lightly grease an 11¼- x 7- x 2-inch ceramic dish. Melt ¾ oz of the butter in a saucepan, add the leek and stir over medium heat for 8 minutes, or until soft. Chop the eggplant and sweet potato into ½-inch thick pieces and place in a bowl. Mix in the leek and one-third of the cheddar.

Melt the remaining butter in a saucepan over medium heat. Stir in the flour and cook for 1 minute, or until foaming. Remove from the heat and gradually stir in the milk. Return to the heat and stir until the sauce boils and thickens. Reduce the heat and simmer for 2 minutes. Season. Stir 1½ cups of the sauce into the vegetable mixture, adding extra if necessary to bind it together.

Cut the lasagne sheets in half widthways to make two smaller rectangles. Spoon the vegetable mixture along the center of one sheet and roll up. Repeat to make 12 tubes in total. Place the tubes, seam-side-down, in the dish and spoon the remaining sauce over the top until they are covered. Sprinkle with the remaining cheese and bake for about 20 minutes, or until the top is golden.

SERVES 4

Ravioli with roasted red pepper sauce

6 red peppers
1 lb 6 oz ravioli
2 tablespoons olive oil
3 garlic cloves, crushed
2 leeks, thinly sliced
1 tablespoon chopped oregano
2 teaspoons brown sugar
1 cup vegetable or chicken stock

Cut the pepper into large flattish pieces and remove the membrane and seeds. Cook, skin side up, under a hot broiler until the skin blackens and blisters. Cool in a plastic bag, then peel the skin.

Cook the pasta in a large saucepan of boiling salted water until *al dente*. Drain well and return to the pan to keep warm.

Meanwhile, heat the olive oil in a frying pan over medium heat. Cook the garlic and leek for 3–4 minutes, or until softened. Add the oregano and brown sugar and stir for 1 minute.

Place the pepper and leek mixture in a food processor or blender, season and process until combined. Add the stock and process until smooth. Gently toss the sauce through the pasta over low heat until warmed through.

SERVES 4

Veal tortellini with baked squash and basil butter

2 lbs 4 oz winter squash, such as jap,
    cut into ¾-inch cubes
1 lb 5 oz veal tortellini
3½ oz butter
3 garlic cloves, crushed
½ cup pine nuts
¾ cup shredded basil
1⅓ cups crumbled feta cheese

Preheat the oven to 425°F. Line a baking tray with baking paper. Place the squash on the prepared tray and season well. Bake for 30 minutes, or until tender.

Meanwhile, cook the pasta in a large saucepan of boiling salted water until *al dente*. Drain well and return to the pan to keep warm.

Heat the butter in a small frying pan over medium heat until foaming. Add the garlic and pine nuts and cook for 3–5 minutes, or until the nuts are starting to turn golden. Remove from the heat and add the basil. Toss the basil butter, squash, and feta through the pasta.

SERVES 4

Roasted chunky
ratatouille cannelloni

1 eggplant
2 zucchini
1 large red pepper
1 large green pepper
3–4 firm, ripe plum tomatoes
12 unpeeled garlic cloves
3 tablespoons olive oil
10½ fl oz puréed tomatoes
12 oz cannelloni tubes
3 tablespoons shredded basil
1¼ cups ricotta cheese
⅔ cup feta cheese
1 egg, lightly beaten
½ cup grated pecorino pepato cheese

Preheat the oven to 400°F. Cut the eggplant, zucchini, peppers, and tomatoes into ¾-inch cubes and place in a baking dish with the garlic. Drizzle with the oil and toss to coat. Bake for 1 hour 30 minutes, or until the vegetables are tender and the tomatoes slightly mushy. Peel and lightly mash the garlic cloves.

Pour the passata over the base of a large ovenproof dish. Spoon the ratatouille into the cannelloni tubes and arrange in the dish.

Combine the basil, ricotta, feta, and egg in a bowl. Season well and spoon over the cannelloni. Sprinkle with the pecorino and bake for 30 minutes, or until the cannelloni is soft.

SERVES 6–8

Salmon and ricotta-stuffed conchiglione

32 conchiglione (about 7 oz)
15 oz canned red salmon, drained,
   bones removed and flaked
2 cups fresh ricotta cheese
1 tablespoon chopped Italian parsley
3 tablespoons chopped chives
1½ celery sticks, finely chopped
¾ cup grated cheddar cheese
¾ cup light whipping cream
3 tablespoons grated parmesan cheese

Preheat the oven to 350°F. Cook the pasta in a large saucepan of boiling salted water until *al dente*. Drain well and return to the pan to keep warm.

Combine the salmon, ricotta, parsley, chives, celery, and cheddar in a bowl and season.

Put 2 teaspoons of filling in each shell. Place the filled shells into a 12 cup ceramic baking dish.

Pour over the cream and sprinkle with the parmesan. Cover with foil and bake for 20 minutes, then remove the foil and bake for a further 15 minutes, or until golden brown. Spoon the cream sauce over the shells and serve.

SERVES 4

Sweet potato ravioli

1 lb 2 oz sweet potato, chopped
2 teaspoons lemon juice
6¾ oz butter
½ cup grated parmesan cheese
1 tablespoon chopped chives
1 egg, lightly beaten
9 oz packet won ton wrappers
2 tablespoons sage, torn
2 tablespoons chopped walnuts

Cook the sweet potato and lemon juice in a large saucepan of boiling water for 15 minutes, or until tender. Drain and pat dry with paper towel. Allow to cool for 5 minutes.

Blend the sweet potato and 1 oz of the butter in a food processor until smooth. Add the parmesan, chives, and half the egg. Season and set aside to cool.

Brush a little of the egg mixture around the edges of half the won ton wrappers. Put 2 teaspoons of the mixture in the center of half the won ton wrappers. Cover with the remaining wrappers and press the edges firmly together. Using a 2¾-inch cutter, cut the ravioli into circles.

Melt the remaining butter in a small saucepan over low heat and cook until golden brown.

Meanwhile, cook the ravioli in a large saucepan of boiling salted water until *al dente*. Remove with a slotted spoon and drain well. Serve immediately, drizzled with the butter and sprinkled with the sage and walnuts.

SERVES 4

Tortellini with speck, asparagus, and tomato

7 oz piece speck (skin removed), roughly chopped
4 firm, ripe tomatoes
14 thin, fresh asparagus spears, cut into 1¼-inch lengths
1 lb 2 oz cheese tortellini
1 tablespoon olive oil
1 red onion, thinly sliced
1 tablespoon concentrated tomato purée
½ cup chicken stock
2 teaspoons thyme leaves

Put the speck in a food processor and pulse until chopped.

Score a cross in the base of the tomatoes. Put in a heatproof bowl and cover with boiling water. Leave for 30 seconds, then transfer to cold water and peel the skin away from the cross. Roughly chop.

Cook the asparagus in a large saucepan of boiling water for 2 minutes, or until just tender. Remove with a slotted spoon and refresh in cold water. Drain. Cook the pasta in the same boiling water and cook until *al dente*. Drain well and return to the pan to keep warm.

Meanwhile, heat the oil in a saucepan over medium heat. Add the speck and onion and cook, stirring, for 2–3 minutes, or until the onion is soft. Add the tomato, tomato purée, stock, and thyme and season. Cook, stirring, for 5 minutes. Add the pasta and asparagus to the tomato mixture and stir over low heat until warmed through.

SERVES 4–6

Agnolotti with creamy sun-dried tomato sauce and bacon

4 bacon slices
1 lb 6 oz veal or chicken agnolotti
1 tablespoon olive oil
2 garlic cloves, finely chopped
²⁄₃ cup thinly sliced sun-dried tomatoes
1 tablespoon chopped thyme
1½ cups light whipping cream
1 teaspoon finely grated lemon zest
4 tablespoons finely grated parmesan cheese

Broil the bacon for 5 minutes on each side, or until crisp and golden. Remove, drain well on paper towel, then break into pieces.

Cook the pasta in a large saucepan of boiling salted water until *al dente*. Drain well and return to the pan to keep warm.

Heat the oil in a frying pan over medium heat. Cook the garlic for 1 minute, or until just golden. Add the tomato and thyme and cook for a further 1 minute.

Add the cream, bring to a boil, then reduce the heat and simmer for 6–8 minutes, or until the cream has thickened and reduced by one-third. Season and add the lemon zest and 2 tablespoons of the parmesan. Pour the sauce over the pasta. Sprinkle with the remaining parmesan and the bacon pieces.

SERVES 4

long

Chili linguine with chermoula chicken

2 large boneless, skinless chicken breasts (about 1 lb 5 oz)
1 lb 2 oz chili linguine

Chermoula
2 cups chopped cilantro leaves
2 cups chopped Italian parsley leaves
4 garlic cloves, crushed
2 teaspoons ground cumin
2 teaspoons ground paprika
½ cup lemon juice
2 teaspoons lemon zest
3½ fl oz olive oil

Heat a large non-stick frying pan over medium heat. Add the chicken breasts and cook until tender. Remove from the pan and leave for 5 minutes before cutting into thin slices.

Cook the pasta in a large saucepan of boiling salted water until *al dente*. Drain well and return to the pan to keep warm.

Meanwhile, combine the chermoula ingredients in a bowl and add the sliced chicken. Serve the pasta topped with the chermoula chicken.

SERVES 4

Spaghettini with anchovies, capers, and chili

14 oz spaghettini
½ cup olive oil
4 garlic cloves, finely chopped
10 anchovy fillets, chopped
1 tablespoon baby capers, rinsed and squeezed dry
1 teaspoon chili flakes
2 tablespoons lemon juice
2 teaspoons finely grated lemon zest
3 tablespoons chopped Italian parsley
3 tablespoons chopped basil
3 tablespoons chopped mint
½ cup coarsely grated parmesan cheese,
    plus extra, to serve
extra virgin olive oil, to drizzle

Cook the pasta in a large saucepan of boiling salted water until *al dente*. Drain well and return to the pan to keep warm.

Heat the oil in a frying pan over medium heat. Cook the garlic for 2–3 minutes, or until starting to brown. Add the anchovies, capers, and chili and cook for 1 minute.

Add the pasta to the pan with the lemon juice, zest, parsley, basil, mint, and parmesan. Season and toss together.

To serve, drizzle with a little extra oil and sprinkle with the parmesan.

SERVES 4

Tagliatelle with beef ragù

3½ oz piece streaky bacon or pancetta (not trimmed),
   finely chopped
1 onion, finely chopped
3 garlic cloves, crushed
1 bay leaf
1 lb 12 oz lean ground beef
2 cups red wine
⅓ cup concentrated tomato purée
14 oz tagliatelle
freshly grated parmesan cheese, to serve

Heat a large deep frying pan over medium–high heat. Add the bacon or pancetta and cook for 2 minutes, or until soft and just starting to brown. Add the onion, garlic, and bay leaf and cook for 2 minutes, or until the onion is soft and just starting to brown.

Add the beef and stir for about 4 minutes or until the beef browns, breaking up any lumps with the back of a wooden spoon. Add the wine, tomato purée, and 1 cup water and stir well. Bring to a boil, then reduce the heat and simmer, covered, for 40 minutes. Remove the lid and cook for a further 40 minutes, or until reduced to a thick sauce.

Meanwhile, cook the pasta in a large saucepan of boiling salted water until *al dente*. Drain well and return to the pan to keep warm.

Serve the sauce over the pasta and top with grated parmesan.

SERVES 4

Spaghetti with clams

2 lbs 4 oz baby clams
13 oz spaghetti
½ cup extra virgin olive oil
1½ oz butter
1 small onion, very finely chopped
6 large garlic cloves, finely chopped
½ cup dry white wine
1 small red chili, seeded and finely chopped
3 tablespoons chopped Italian parsley

Scrub the clams with a small stiff brush to remove any grit, discarding any that are open or cracked. Soak and rinse the clams in several changes of water over 1 hour, or until the water is clean and free of grit. Drain and set aside.

Cook the pasta in a large saucepan of boiling salted water until *al dente*. Drain well and return to the pan to keep warm.

Heat the oil and 1 tablespoon of the butter in a large saucepan over medium heat. Add the onion and half the garlic and cook for 10 minutes, or until lightly golden. Add the wine and cook for 2 minutes. Add the clams, chili, and the remaining butter and garlic. Cook, covered, for 8 minutes, shaking regularly, until the clams pop open. Discard any that are still closed.

Stir in the parsley and season. Add the pasta and toss together.

SERVES 4

Pasta alla Norma

¾ cup olive oil
1 onion, finely chopped
2 garlic cloves, finely chopped
1 lb 12 oz canned chopped tomatoes
14 oz bucatini
1 large eggplant, about 1 lb 2 oz
½ cup torn basil leaves, plus extra, to garnish
½ cup ricotta salata (see Note), crumbled
½ cup grated pecorino or parmesan cheese
1 tablespoon extra virgin olive oil, to drizzle

Heat 2 tablespoons of the oil in a frying pan over medium heat. Cook the onion for 5 minutes, or until softened. Stir in the garlic and cook for 30 seconds. Add the tomato and season. Reduce the heat to low and cook for 20–25 minutes, or until the sauce has thickened and reduced.

Cook the pasta in a large saucepan of boiling salted water until *al dente*. Drain well and return to the pan to keep warm.

Meanwhile, cut the eggplant lengthways into ¼-inch thick slices. Heat the remaining olive oil in a large frying pan over medium heat. Add the eggplant slices a few at a time and cook for 3–5 minutes, or until lightly browned on both sides. Remove from the pan and drain on crumpled paper towel.

Add the eggplant to the sauce with the basil, stirring over very low heat. Add the pasta to the sauce with half each of the ricotta and pecorino and toss together. Serve sprinkled with the remaining cheeses and basil and drizzle with oil.

SERVES 4–6

NOTE: Ricotta salata is a lightly salted, pressed ricotta cheese. If unavailable, use a mild feta cheese.

Creamy tomato and shrimp tagliatelle

14 oz dried egg tagliatelle
1 tablespoon olive oil
3 garlic cloves, finely chopped
20 medium raw shrimp, peeled and deveined,
    with tails intact
6 plum tomatoes, diced
2 tablespoons thinly sliced basil
½ cup white wine
4 tablespoons light whipping cream
basil leaves, to garnish

Cook the pasta in a large saucepan of boiling salted water until *al dente*. Drain well, reserving 2 tablespoons of the cooking water. Return the pasta to the pan to keep warm.

Meanwhile, heat the oil and garlic in a large frying pan over low heat for 1–2 minutes. Increase the heat to medium, add the shrimp and cook for 3–5 minutes, stirring frequently until cooked. Remove the shrimp and keep warm.

Add the tomato and sliced basil and stir for 3 minutes, or until the tomato is soft. Pour in the wine and cream, bring to a boil and simmer for 2 minutes.

Purée the sauce in a blender. Return to the pan, then add the reserved pasta water and bring to a simmer. Stir in the shrimp until heated through. Toss through the pasta and serve garnished with the basil leaves.

SERVES 4

Bavette with chicken, pine nuts, and lemon

3 lbs whole chicken
1 garlic bulb, cloves separated
    and left unpeeled
3 tablespoons olive oil
1 oz butter, softened
1 tablespoon finely chopped
    thyme
½ cup lemon juice
1 lb 2 oz bavette or spaghetti

2 tablespoons currants
1 teaspoon finely grated lemon
    zest
⅓ cup pine nuts, toasted
½ cup finely chopped
    Italian parsley

Preheat the oven to 400°F. Remove the neck from the inside of the chicken and place the neck in a roasting tin. Rinse the inside of the chicken with cold water. Insert the garlic cloves into the cavity, then put the chicken in the tin.

Combine the oil, butter, thyme, and lemon juice, then rub over the chicken. Season. Roast for 1 hour, or until the skin is golden and the juices run clear when the thigh is pierced with a skewer. Transfer the chicken to a bowl. Remove the garlic from the cavity, cool, then squeeze the garlic cloves out of their skins and finely chop.

Cook the pasta in a large saucepan of boiling salted water until *al dente*. Drain well and return to the pan to keep warm.

Meanwhile, pour the juices from the roasting tin into a saucepan and discard the neck. Add the currants, zest, and chopped garlic, then simmer over low heat. Remove all the meat from the chicken and shred. Add the resting juices to the pan. Add the chicken, pine nuts, parsley, and sauce to the pasta and toss.

SERVES 4–6

Fettucine with creamy spinach and roast tomato

6 plum tomatoes
1½ oz butter
2 garlic cloves, crushed
1 onion, chopped
1 lb 2 oz spinach, trimmed
1 cup vegetable stock
½ cup heavy whipping cream
1 lb 2 oz fresh spinach fettucine
½ cup shaved parmesan cheese

Preheat the oven to 425°F. Cut the tomatoes in half lengthways,
then cut each half into three wedges. Place the wedges on a lightly greased baking
tray and roast for 30–35 minutes, or until softened and slightly golden.

Meanwhile, heat the butter in a large frying pan over medium heat. Add the garlic
and onion and cook for 5 minutes, or until the onion is soft. Add the spinach, stock,
and cream. Increase the heat to high and bring to a boil. Simmer for 5 minutes.
Remove from the heat and season. Set aside to cool slightly.

Meanwhile, cook the pasta in a large saucepan of boiling salted water until *al dente*.
Drain well and return to the pan to keep warm.

Process the spinach mixture in a food processor until smooth. Toss through the
pasta until well coated. Top with the roasted tomatoes and parmesan.

SERVES 4–6

Spaghettini with squid in black ink

2 lbs 4 oz squid
2 tablespoons olive oil
1 onion, finely chopped
6 garlic cloves, finely chopped
1 bay leaf
1 small red chili, seeded and
 thinly sliced
4 tablespoons white wine
4 tablespoons dry vermouth
1 cup fish stock

3 tablespoons concentrated
 tomato purée
2 cups puréed tomatoes
½ oz squid ink
1 lb 2 oz spaghettini
½ teaspoon Pernod (optional)
4 tablespoons chopped Italian
 parsley
1 garlic clove, extra, crushed

To clean the squid, gently pull the tentacles away from the tube. Remove the intestines from the tentacles by cutting under the eyes, then remove the beak if it remains in the center of the tentacles by using your fingers to push up the center. Pull away the quill from inside the body and remove. Remove and discard any white membrane. Pull away the skin from the hood. Slice the squid into rings.

Heat the oil in a saucepan over medium heat. Add the onion and cook until golden. Add the garlic, bay leaf, and chili and cook for 2 minutes. Stir in the wine, vermouth, stock, tomato purée, puréed tomatoes and 1 cup water. Increase the heat to high and bring to a boil. Reduce to a simmer. Cook for 45 minutes, or until the liquid has reduced by half. Add the squid ink and cook for 2 minutes.

Meanwhile, cook the pasta in a large saucepan of boiling salted water until *al dente*. Drain and return to the pan. Add the squid rings and Pernod. Cook for 4 minutes, or until cooked through. Stir in the parsley and the extra garlic and season.

SERVES 4–6

Summer seafood marinara

10½ oz fresh saffron angel hair pasta
1 tablespoon extra virgin olive oil
1 oz butter
2 garlic cloves, finely chopped
1 large onion, finely chopped
1 small red chili, finely chopped
1 lb 5 oz canned peeled tomatoes, chopped
1 cup white wine
zest of 1 lemon
½ tablespoon sugar
7 oz scallops without roe
1 lb 2 oz raw shrimp, peeled and deveined
10½ oz clams

Cook the pasta in a large saucepan of boiling salted water until *al dente*. Drain well and return to the pan to keep warm.

Heat the oil and butter in a large frying pan over medium heat. Add the garlic, onion, and chili and cook for 5 minutes, or until soft. Add the tomatoes and wine and bring to a boil. Cook for 10 minutes, or until the sauce has reduced and thickened slightly.

Add the lemon zest, sugar, scallops, shrimp, and clams. Cook, covered, for 5 minutes, or until the seafood is tender. Discard any clams that do not open. Season and serve the pasta topped with the sauce.

SERVES 4

Spicy eggplant
spaghetti

10½ oz spaghetti
½ cup extra virgin olive oil
2 red chilies, finely sliced
1 onion, finely chopped
3 garlic cloves, crushed
4 bacon slices, chopped
1 large eggplant, diced
2 tablespoons balsamic vinegar
2 tomatoes, chopped
3 tablespoons shredded basil

Cook the pasta in a large saucepan of boiling salted water until *al dente*. Drain well and return to the pan to keep warm.

Heat 1 tablespoon of the oil in a large, deep frying pan over medium heat. Cook the chili, onion, garlic, and bacon for 5 minutes, or until the onion is golden and the bacon browned. Remove from the pan and set aside.

Add half the remaining oil to the pan and cook half the eggplant over high heat, tossing to brown on all sides. Remove and repeat with the remaining oil and eggplant. Return the bacon mixture and all the eggplant to the pan, add the vinegar, tomato, and basil and cook until heated through. Season.

Serve the spaghetti topped with the eggplant mixture.

SERVES 4

Pastitsio

2 tablespoons oil
4 garlic cloves, crushed
2 onions, chopped
2 lbs 4 oz ground beef
2 lbs 4 oz canned peeled
    tomatoes, chopped
1 cup dry red wine
1 cup beef stock
1 bay leaf
1 teaspoon dried mixed herbs
12 oz ziti

3 eggs, lightly beaten
2 cups Greek-style yogurt
2 cups grated kefalotyri cheese
    (or other salty, hard sheep's
    cheese)
½ teaspoon ground nutmeg
½ cup grated cheddar cheese
oakleaf lettuce, to serve

Heat the oil in a large heavy-based frying pan over medium heat. Cook the garlic and onion for 5 minutes, or until the onion is soft. Add the beef and cook over high heat until browned, then drain off any excess fat. Add the tomato, wine, stock, bay leaf, and herbs and bring to a boil. Reduce the heat and simmer for 40 minutes. Season well.

Preheat the oven to 350°F. Meanwhile, cook the pasta in a large saucepan of boiling salted water until *al dente*. Drain well and spread in the base of a large ovenproof dish. Pour in half the egg and top with the sauce.

Combine the yogurt, remaining egg, kefalotyri, and nutmeg and pour over the top. Sprinkle with the cheddar and bake for 40 minutes, or until golden brown. Serve with oakleaf lettuce.

SERVES 6–8

Spaghetti puttanesca

14 oz spaghetti
2 tablespoons olive oil
1 onion, finely chopped
2 garlic cloves, finely sliced
1 small red chili, cored, seeded and sliced
6 anchovy fillets, finely chopped
14 oz canned chopped tomatoes
1 tablespoon fresh oregano, finely chopped
16 black olives, halved and pitted
2 tablespoons baby capers
1 handful basil leaves

Cook the pasta in a large saucepan of boiling salted water until *al dente*. Drain well and return to the pan to keep warm.

Heat the olive oil in a large saucepan over medium heat. Add the onion, garlic, and chili and cook for 8 minutes, or until the onion is soft. Add the anchovies and cook for a further 1 minute. Add the tomato, oregano, olive halves, and capers and bring to a boil. Reduce the heat, season and simmer for 3 minutes.

Add the spaghetti to the sauce and toss together. Scatter the basil over the top.

SERVES 4

Spaghettini with asparagus and arugula

3½ fl oz extra virgin olive oil
16 thin, fresh asparagus spears, cut into 2-inch lengths
13 oz spaghettini
2⅔ cups shredded arugula
2 small red chilies, finely chopped
2 teaspoons finely grated lemon zest
1 garlic clove, finely chopped
1 cup grated parmesan cheese
2 tablespoons lemon juice

Bring a large saucepan of water to a boil over medium heat. Add 1 tablespoon of the oil and a pinch of salt to the water and blanch the asparagus for 3–4 minutes. Remove the asparagus with a slotted spoon, refresh under cold water, drain and place in a bowl. Return the water to a rapid boil and add the spaghettini. Cook the pasta until *al dente*. Drain well and return to the pan to keep warm.

Meanwhile, add the arugula, chili, lemon zest, garlic, and ⅔ cup of the parmesan to the asparagus and mix well. Add to the pasta, pour on the lemon juice and remaining olive oil and season. Stir well to combine. Top with the remaining parmesan.

SERVES 4

Paprika veal with caraway fettuccine

3 tablespoons oil
2 lbs 4 oz diced veal shoulder
1 large onion, thinly sliced
3 garlic cloves, finely chopped
3 tablespoons paprika
1/2 teaspoon caraway seeds
1 lb 12 oz canned chopped tomatoes, half drained
12 oz fettuccine
1 1/2 oz butter, softened

Heat half the oil in a large saucepan over medium–high heat. Brown the veal in batches for 3 minutes per batch. Remove the veal from the pan and set aside with any pan juices.

Add the remaining oil to the pan and sauté the onion and garlic over medium heat for 5 minutes, or until softened. Add the paprika and 1/4 teaspoon of the caraway seeds and stir for 30 seconds.

Add the chopped tomatoes and their liquid plus 1/2 cup water. Return the veal to the pan with any juices, increase the heat to high and bring to a boil. Reduce the heat to low, then cover and simmer for 1 hour 15 minutes, or until the meat is tender and the sauce has thickened.

Meanwhile, cook the pasta in a large saucepan of boiling salted water until *al dente*. Drain well and return to the pan to keep warm.

Stir in the butter and the remaining caraway seeds. Serve immediately with the veal.

SERVES 4

Buckwheat pasta
with cabbage, potato, and cheese sauce

12 oz savoy cabbage, roughly chopped
6 oz potatoes, cut into ¾-inch cubes
1 lb 2 oz buckwheat pasta (see Note)
4 tablespoons extra virgin olive oil
1 oz sage, finely chopped
2 garlic cloves, finely chopped
12 oz mixed cheeses (such as mascarpone,
    fontina, taleggio, and gorgonzola)
grated parmesan cheese, to serve

Bring a large saucepan of salted water to a boil. Add the cabbage, potato, and the pasta and cook for 3–5 minutes, or until the pasta is *al dente* and the vegetables are cooked. Drain well, reserving about 1 cup of the cooking water.

Add the olive oil to the saucepan and gently cook the sage and garlic for about 1 minute. Add the mixed cheeses to the pan. Stir, then add the pasta, cabbage, and potatoes. Season. Remove the saucepan from the heat and gently stir the mixture together, adding some of the reserved pasta water to loosen it up a little if necessary. Serve with parmesan.

SERVES 6

NOTE: Buckwheat pasta is called pizzoccheri in Italy. This type of pasta is popular in Valtellina, near the Swiss border, and is traditionally served with potatoes, cabbage, and cheese.

Spaghetti Bolognese

2¼ oz butter
1 onion, finely chopped
2 garlic cloves, crushed
1 celery stick, finely chopped
1 carrot, diced
1¾ oz piece pancetta, diced
1 lb 2 oz ground beef
1 tablespoon chopped oregano
1 cup dry red wine
2 cups beef stock
2 tablespoons concentrated tomato purée
1 lb 12 oz canned crushed tomatoes
14 oz spaghetti
3 tablespoons grated parmesan cheese

Melt the butter in a large saucepan over medium heat. Add the onion and cook for 2–3 minutes, or until soft. Add the garlic, celery, and carrot, and cook, stirring, over low heat, for 5 minutes. Increase the heat to high, add the pancetta, beef, and oregano, and cook for 4–5 minutes or until browned.

Pour in the wine, reduce the heat and simmer for 4–5 minutes, or until absorbed. Add the stock, tomato purée, and tomatoes and season. Cover with a lid and simmer for 1½ hours, stirring occasionally. Uncover and simmer for a further 1 hour, stirring occasionally.

Cook the pasta in a large saucepan of boiling salted water until *al dente*. Drain well and return to the pan to keep warm.

Top the pasta with the sauce. Serve with the parmesan.

SERVES 4

Ziti carbonara

1 tablespoon olive oil
7 oz piece pancetta, cut into long thin strips
1 lb 2 oz ziti
4 egg yolks
10½ fl oz light whipping cream
½ cup grated parmesan cheese, plus extra to serve
2 tablespoons finely chopped Italian parsley

Heat the olive oil in a non-stick frying pan over high heat. Cook the pancetta for 6 minutes, or until crisp and golden.

Meanwhile, cook the pasta in a large saucepan of boiling salted water until *al dente*. Drain well and return to the pan to keep warm.

Beat the egg yolks, cream, and parmesan together in a bowl and season. Pour over the pasta in the saucepan and toss. Add the pancetta and parsley. Cook over very low heat for 30–60 seconds, or until the sauce has thickened and coats the pasta. Don't overheat or the eggs will scramble. Season and serve with extra parmesan.

SERVES 4–6

Tagliatelle with tuna, capers, and arugula

3 garlic cloves, crushed
1 teaspoon finely grated lemon zest
4 tablespoons extra virgin olive oil
1 lb 2 oz tuna, cut into ½-inch cubes
12 oz fresh tagliatelle
4½ cups roughly chopped arugula
4 tablespoons baby capers in salt, rinsed and squeezed dry
3 tablespoons lemon juice
2 tablespoons finely chopped Italian parsley

Combine the garlic, lemon zest, 1 tablespoon of the oil, and the tuna in a bowl and season.

Meanwhile, cook the pasta in a large saucepan of boiling salted water until *al dente*. Drain well and return to the pan to keep warm.

Heat a non-stick frying pan over high heat. Sear the tuna for 30 seconds on each side. Add the arugula and capers and gently stir for 1 minute, or until the arugula has just wilted. Pour in the lemon juice and then remove from the heat.

Add the remaining oil, tuna mixture, and parsley to the pasta. Season and toss.

SERVES 4

Creamy garlic shrimp fettuccine

14 oz fresh fettuccine
1 tablespoon olive oil
1 onion, finely chopped
3 garlic cloves, crushed
14 oz firm, ripe tomatoes, seeded and chopped
3 tablespoons white wine
10½ fl oz light whipping cream
2 lbs 4 oz raw shrimp, peeled and deveined, with
   tails intact
3 tablespoons roughly chopped basil

Cook the pasta in a large saucepan of boiling salted water until *al dente*. Drain well and return to the pan to keep warm.

Heat the oil in a large frying pan over medium–high heat. Cook the onion and garlic, stirring, for 4–5 minutes, or until the onion is soft. Add the tomato and wine and cook for 3 minutes, then add the cream. Bring to the boil, then reduce the heat to medium–low and simmer for 5 minutes, or until it slightly thickens.

Stir in the shrimp, then simmer for 3–4 minutes, or until the shrimp turn pink and are curled and cooked through. Toss with the pasta, stir in the basil and season.

SERVES 4

Spaghetti with meatballs

Meatballs

1 lb 2 oz ground beef
½ cup fresh breadcrumbs
1 onion, finely chopped
2 garlic cloves, crushed
2 teaspoons worcestershire
   sauce
1 teaspoon dried oregano
3 tablespoons all-purpose flour
2 tablespoons olive oil

Sauce

1 lb 12 oz canned chopped
   tomatoes
1 tablespoon olive oil
1 onion, finely chopped
2 garlic cloves, crushed
2 tablespoons concentrated
   tomato purée
4 fl oz beef stock
2 teaspoons sugar

1 lb 2 oz spaghetti
grated parmesan cheese,
   to serve

Combine the beef, breadcrumbs, onion, garlic, worcestershire sauce, and oregano in a bowl and season. Mix well. Roll level tablespoons of the mixture into balls, dust with the flour and shake off the excess. Heat the oil in a frying pan over high heat. Cook the meatballs in batches, turning, until browned all over. Drain well.

Purée the tomatoes in a food processor. Heat the oil in a frying pan over medium heat. Add the onion and cook until soft. Add the garlic and cook for 1 minute. Add the puréed tomatoes, tomato purée, stock, and sugar and stir to combine. Bring to a boil and add the meatballs. Reduce the heat and simmer for 15 minutes. Season.

Meanwhile, cook the pasta in a large saucepan of boiling salted water until *al dente*.

Spaghetti marinara

Tomato sauce
2 tablespoons olive oil
1 onion, finely chopped
1 carrot, finely chopped
2 garlic cloves, crushed
14 oz canned chopped tomatoes
½ cup white wine
1 teaspoon sugar

3 tablespoons white wine
3 tablespoons fish stock
1 garlic clove, crushed
12 black mussels, cleaned

13 oz spaghetti
1 oz butter
4½ oz squid, cleaned and cut
　　into rings
4½ oz skinless cod fillet, cut into
　　bite-sized pieces
7 oz shrimp, peeled and
　　deveined
1 handful Italian parsley,
　　chopped
7 oz canned clams, drained

Heat the oil in a saucepan over medium heat. Cook the onion and carrot for 10 minutes, or until browned. Add the garlic, tomato, wine, and sugar. Bring to a boil, then reduce the heat and simmer for 30 minutes, stirring occasionally.

Heat the wine, stock, and garlic in a large saucepan over high heat. Add the mussels. Cover and shake the pan for 5 minutes. Discard any unopened mussels and reserve the cooking liquid.

Cook the pasta in a large saucepan of boiling salted water until *al dente*. Drain well and return to the pan to keep warm.

Melt the butter in a frying pan over medium heat. Stir-fry the squid, cod, and shrimp in batches for 2 minutes, or until just cooked. Add to the tomato sauce along with the reserved cooking liquid, mussels, parsley, and clams. Toss together.

SERVES 4

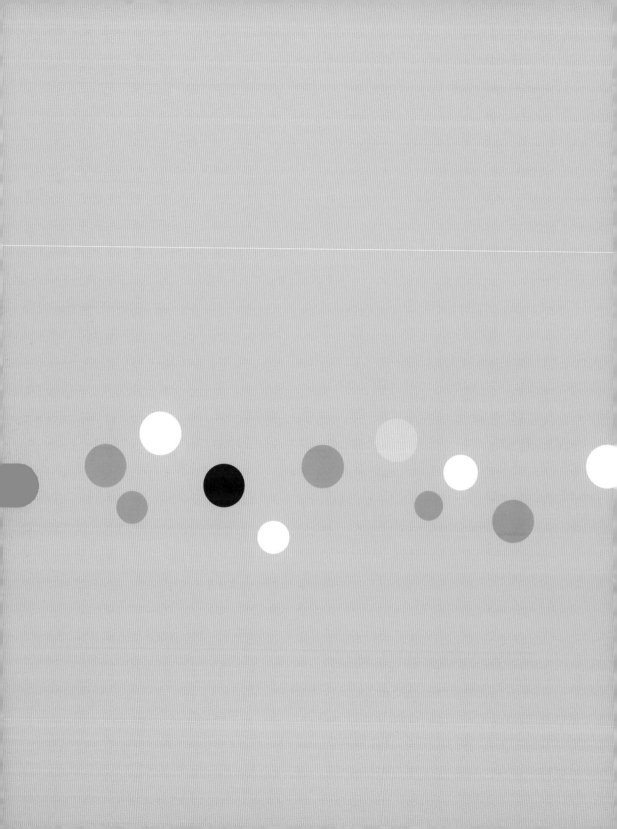

curly

Fusilli with roasted tomatoes, tapenade, and bocconcini

1 lb 12 oz cherry or teardrop tomatoes
   (or a mixture of both), halved if they are large
1 lb 2 oz fusilli
10½ oz bocconcini, sliced
1 tablespoon chopped thyme

Tapenade
1½ tablespoons capers, rinsed and squeezed dry
2 small garlic cloves
1½ cups sliced black olives
3 tablespoons lemon juice
4–5 tablespoons extra virgin olive oil

Preheat the oven to 400°F. Place the tomatoes on a baking tray, season and roast for 10 minutes, or until slightly dried.

To make the tapenade, put the capers, garlic, olives, and lemon juice in a food processor and mix together. With the motor running, gradually add the oil until the mixture forms a smooth paste.

Cook the pasta in a large saucepan of boiling salted water until *al dente*. Drain well and return to the pan to keep warm. Toss the tapenade and bocconcini through the pasta. Top with the tomatoes and thyme.

SERVES 4–6

Warm minted chicken and cotelli salad

9 oz cotelli
½ cup olive oil
1 large red pepper
3 boneless, skinless chicken
   breasts
6 scallions, cut into
   ¾-inch lengths

4 garlic cloves, thinly sliced
¾ cup chopped mint
4 tablespoons cider vinegar
2 cups baby spinach leaves

Cook the pasta in a large saucepan of boiling salted water until *al dente*. Drain well and return to the pan to keep warm. Stir in 1 tablespoon of the oil.

Meanwhile, cut the pepper into quarters and remove the membrane and seeds. Cook, skin side up, under a hot broiler until the skin blackens and blisters. Cool in a plastic bag, then peel the skin. Cut into thin strips.

Put the chicken between two sheets of plastic wrap and press with the palm of your hand until slightly flattened.

Heat 1 tablespoon of the oil in a large frying pan over medium heat. Add the chicken and cook for 2–3 minutes each side, or until cooked through. Remove from the pan and cut into ¼-inch thick slices.

Add 1 tablespoon of the oil to the pan and add the scallions, garlic, and pepper. Cook, stirring, for 2–3 minutes, or until starting to soften. Add two-thirds of the mint, the vinegar, and the remaining oil and stir.

Combine the pasta, chicken, spinach, scallion mixture, and remaining mint. Toss together and season.

SERVES 4

Prosciutto and vegetable pasta bake

3 tablespoons olive oil
4 tablespoons dry breadcrumbs
3¼ cups mixed curly pasta, such
   as cotelli and fusilli
6 thin slices prosciutto, chopped
1 red onion, chopped
1 red pepper, chopped
⅔ cup chopped sun-dried
   tomatoes

3 tablespoons shredded basil
1 cup grated parmesan cheese
4 eggs, lightly beaten
1 cup milk

Preheat the oven to 350°F. Lightly grease a 10-inch round ovenproof dish. Sprinkle the dish with 2 tablespoons of the breadcrumbs to coat the base and side.

Cook the pasta in a large saucepan of boiling water until *al dente*. Drain well and return to the pan to keep warm.

Heat 1 tablespoon of the oil in a large frying pan over medium heat. Add the prosciutto and onion and cook for 4–5 minutes, or until softened. Add the pepper and sun-dried tomato and cook for a further 1–2 minutes. Add to the pasta with the basil and parmesan and toss. Spoon into the prepared dish.

Place the eggs and milk in a bowl, whisk together, then season. Pour the egg mixture over the pasta. Season the remaining breadcrumbs, add the remaining oil and toss together. Sprinkle the seasoned breadcrumb mixture over the pasta. Bake for 40 minutes, or until set. Cut into wedges to serve.

SERVES 6–8

Cotelli with spring vegetables

1 lb 2 oz cotelli
2 cups frozen peas
2 cups frozen fava beans, blanched and peeled
4 tablespoons olive oil
6 scallions, cut into 1¼-inch pieces
2 garlic cloves, finely chopped
1 cup chicken stock
12 thin, fresh asparagus spears, cut into 2-inch lengths
1 lemon

Cook the pasta in a large saucepan of boiling salted water until *al dente*. Drain well and return to the pan to keep warm.

Meanwhile, cook the peas in a saucepan of boiling water for 1–2 minutes, until tender. Remove with a slotted spoon and plunge into cold water. Drain well. Add the fava beans to the saucepan, cook for 1–2 minutes, then drain and plunge into cold water. Remove and slip the skins off.

Heat 2 tablespoons of the olive oil in a frying pan over medium heat. Add the scallions and garlic and cook for 2 minutes, or until softened. Pour in the stock and cook for 5 minutes, or until slightly reduced. Add the asparagus and cook for 3–4 minutes, or until bright green and just tender. Stir in the peas and fava beans and cook for 2–3 minutes, or until heated through.

Toss the remaining oil through the pasta. Add the vegetable mixture, ½ teaspoon finely grated lemon zest and 3 tablespoons lemon juice. Season and toss together.

SERVES 4

Fusilli salad with sherry vinaigrette

10½ oz fusilli
2 cups cauliflower florets
½ cup olive oil
16 slices pancetta
  (about 5¾ oz)
1 handful small sage leaves
⅔ cup pine nuts, toasted
2 tablespoons finely chopped
  shallots

1½ tablespoons sherry vinegar
1 small red chili, finely chopped
2 garlic cloves, crushed
1 teaspoon soft brown sugar
2 tablespoons orange juice
1 handful Italian parsley, finely
  chopped
4 tablespoons shaved parmesan
  cheese

Cook the pasta in a large saucepan of boiling salted water until *al dente*. Drain and refresh under cold water. Drain well. Blanch the cauliflower florets in boiling water for 3 minutes, then drain and allow to cool.

Heat 1 tablespoon of the olive oil in a non-stick frying pan over medium heat and cook the pancetta for 2 minutes, or until crisp. Drain on paper towel.

Add another 1 tablespoon of oil and cook the sage leaves for 1 minute, or until crisp. Drain on paper towel. Combine the pasta, pine nuts, and cauliflower in a bowl.

Heat the remaining olive oil. Add the shallots and cook gently for 2 minutes, or until soft. Remove from the heat, then add the vinegar, chili, garlic, brown sugar, orange juice, and chopped parsley. Pour the warm dressing over the pasta and toss gently to combine.

Crumble the pancetta over the top and scatter with sage leaves and shaved parmesan. Serve warm.

SERVES 6

Cresti di gallo
with creamy tomato and bacon sauce

14 oz cresti di gallo (see Note)
1 tablespoon olive oil
3 thin bacon slices
6 plum tomatoes, roughly chopped
½ cup light whipping cream
2 tablespoons sun-dried tomato pesto
2 tablespoons finely chopped Italian parsley
½ cup finely grated parmesan cheese

Cook the pasta in a large saucepan of boiling salted water until *al dente*. Drain well and return to the pan to keep warm.

Meanwhile, heat the oil in a frying pan over high heat. Add the bacon and cook for 2 minutes, or until starting to brown. Reduce the heat to medium. Add the tomato and cook, stirring frequently, for 2 minutes, or until the tomato has softened but still holds its shape.

Add the cream and tomato pesto and stir until heated through. Remove from the heat. Add the parsley, then toss the sauce through the pasta with the parmesan.

SERVES 4

NOTE: Cresti di gallo pasta is named after the Italian word for 'cockscombs' because of its similarity to the crest of a rooster. You can also use cotelli or fusilli.

Fusilli with tuna, capers, and parsley

15 oz canned tuna in springwater, drained
2 tablespoons olive oil
2 garlic cloves, finely chopped
2 small red chilies, finely chopped
3 tablespoons capers, rinsed and squeezed dry
½ cup chopped Italian parsley
3 tablespoons lemon juice
13 oz fusilli
½ cup chicken stock

Put the tuna in a bowl and flake lightly with a fork. Combine the oil, garlic, chili, capers, parsley, and lemon juice in a small bowl. Pour the mixture over the tuna and mix. Season.

Meanwhile, cook the pasta in a large saucepan of boiling salted water until *al dente*. Drain well and return to the pan to keep warm.

Toss the tuna mixture through the pasta, adding enough of the hot chicken stock to make it moist.

SERVES 4

Peppered pork, zucchini, and garganelli

1 lb pork fillet
3–4 teaspoons cracked black peppercorns
2¾ oz butter
9 oz garganelli
1 onion, halved and thinly sliced
2 large zucchini, thinly sliced
1 large handful basil, torn
¾ cup small black olives
½ cup grated romano cheese

Cut the pork fillet in half widthways and roll in the pepper and some salt. Heat half the butter in a large deep frying pan over medium heat. Add the pork and cook for 4 minutes on each side, or until golden brown and just cooked through. Remove from the pan and cut into ¼-inch thick slices, then set aside and keep warm.

Cook the pasta in a large saucepan of boiling salted water until *al dente*. Drain well and return to the pan to keep warm.

Meanwhile, melt the remaining butter in the frying pan over medium heat. Add the onion and cook, stirring, for about 3 minutes, or until soft. Add the zucchini and toss for 5 minutes, or until starting to soften. Add the basil, olives, sliced pork, and any juices and toss well. Stir the pork mixture through the pasta, then season. Serve topped with the romano cheese.

SERVES 4

Cotelli, tomato, and artichoke broil

12 oz cotelli
10 oz jar marinated artichoke hearts,
   drained and chopped
2 tablespoons olive oil
1 cup light whipping cream
2 tablespoons chopped thyme
2 garlic cloves, crushed
¾ cup grated parmesan cheese
1⅔ cups grated cheddar cheese
8 medium tomatoes, cut into ¼-inch thick slices

Cook the pasta in a large saucepan of boiling salted water until *al dente*. Drain well and return to the pan to keep warm.

Lightly grease a 9- x 12-inch rectangular ovenproof dish. Stir the artichokes, olive oil, cream, thyme, garlic, half the parmesan, and 1¼ cups of the cheddar through the pasta and season. Spread evenly in the dish.

Arrange the tomatoes over the top, overlapping one another. Season, then sprinkle with the remaining cheese. Cook under a hot broiler for 6 minutes, or until the cheeses melt and are golden brown.

SERVES 4

Fusilli with chicken, mushroom, and tarragon

13 oz fusilli
2 tablespoons olive oil
8 chicken tenderloins, cut into ¾-inch thick pieces
¾ oz butter
14 oz brown or button mushrooms, sliced
2 garlic cloves, finely chopped
½ cup dry white wine
¾ cup light whipping cream
1 teaspoon finely grated lemon zest
2 tablespoons lemon juice
1 tablespoon chopped tarragon
2 tablespoons chopped Italian parsley
3 tablespoons grated parmesan cheese, plus extra, to serve

Cook the pasta in a large saucepan of boiling salted water until *al dente*. Drain well and return to the pan to keep warm.

Meanwhile, heat 1 tablespoon of the oil in a large frying pan over high heat. Add the chicken and cook for 3–4 minutes, or until lightly browned. Remove from the pan.

Heat the butter and the remaining oil in the frying pan over high heat. Add the mushrooms and cook for 3 minutes. Add the garlic and cook for a further 2 minutes.

Pour in the wine, then reduce the heat to low and simmer for 5 minutes. Add the cream and chicken and simmer for about 5 minutes, or until thickened. Stir in the lemon zest, lemon juice, tarragon, parsley, and parmesan. Season, then add the pasta, tossing until well combined. Serve with the extra parmesan.

SERVES 4

Fusilli with broccolini, chili, and olives

3 tablespoons olive oil
1 onion, finely chopped
3 garlic cloves
1 teaspoon chili flakes
1 lb 9 oz broccolini, cut into ½-inch thick pieces
½ cup vegetable stock
14 oz fusilli
½ cup black olives, pitted and chopped
1 handful Italian parsley, finely chopped
3 tablespoons grated pecorino cheese
2 tablespoons basil leaves, shredded

Heat the olive oil in a large non-stick frying pan over medium heat. Cook the onion, garlic, and chili until softened. Add the broccolini and cook for 5 minutes. Pour in the stock and cook, covered, for 5 minutes.

Meanwhile, cook the pasta in a large saucepan of boiling salted water until *al dente*. Drain well and return to the pan to keep warm.

When the broccolini is tender, remove from the heat. Add to the pasta with the olives, parsley, pecorino, and basil, and season. Toss together to combine.

SERVES 4

Goulash with fusilli

14 oz fusilli
2 tablespoons olive oil
1 large onion, sliced into thin wedges
1 lb 5 oz rump steak, trimmed and cut into
    ¾-inch cubes
1 tablespoon all-purpose flour
1 small green pepper, diced
1 lb 14 oz canned diced tomatoes
1 teaspoon hot paprika
4 tablespoons light sour cream

Cook the pasta in a large saucepan of boiling salted water until *al dente*. Drain well and return to the pan to keep warm.

Meanwhile, heat 1 tablespoon of the olive oil in a large frying pan over medium heat. Add the onion and cook, stirring, for 4–5 minutes, or until softened and golden. Remove the onion from the pan.

Heat the remaining olive oil in the same frying pan over high heat. Toss the steak cubes in the flour, shaking off any excess, then add to the pan and cook for 2 minutes to brown on all sides. Add the pepper, tomato, paprika, and the cooked onion and stir to combine.

Bring the mixture to a boil, then reduce the heat and simmer for 8–10 minutes, stirring occasionally. Season. To serve, spoon the goulash mixture over the pasta and top with sour cream.

SERVES 4

Sweet potato, arugula, and walnut pasta salad

1 large sweet potato, cut into
  ¾-inch cubes
5 fl oz olive oil
1 cup walnut pieces
12 oz fricelli
5½ oz white castello cheese (or other creamy soft-rind cheese),
  softened
2 garlic cloves, crushed
2 teaspoons lemon juice
½ teaspoon sugar
2¼ cups baby arugula

Preheat the oven to 400°F. Toss the sweet potato in 2 tablespoons of the oil and place in a single layer on a baking tray lined with baking paper. Season. Roast, turning halfway through, for 30 minutes, or until golden and cooked through.

Spread the walnuts on a baking tray and roast for 10 minutes, or until crisp.

Meanwhile, cook the pasta in a large saucepan of boiling salted water until *al dente*. Drain well and return to the pan to keep warm.

Remove the rind from one-third of the cheese and cut the rest into cubes. Finely chop 2 tablespoons of the walnuts. Combine with the garlic, lemon juice, sugar, remaining oil, and rindless cheese. Season. Combine the pasta, sweet potato, arugula, cubed cheese, and remaining walnuts in a bowl. Drizzle with the dressing and toss together. Season.

SERVES 4

Chicken, broccoli, and pasta bake

10½ oz fusilli
15 oz canned cream of mushroom soup
2 eggs
¾ cup whole-egg mayonnaise
1 tablespoon dijon mustard
1⅔ cups grated cheddar cheese
2 large boneless, skinless chicken breasts, thinly sliced
14 oz frozen broccoli pieces, thawed
½ cup fresh breadcrumbs

Preheat the oven to 350°F. Cook the pasta in a large saucepan of boiling salted water until *al dente*. Drain well and return to the pan to keep warm.

Combine the soup, eggs, mayonnaise, mustard, and half the cheese in a bowl.

Heat a lightly greased non-stick frying pan over medium heat. Add the chicken pieces and cook for 5–6 minutes, or until cooked through. Season, then set aside to cool.

Add the chicken and broccoli to the pasta. Pour the soup mixture over the top and stir until well combined. Transfer the mixture to a 12-cup ovenproof dish. Sprinkle with the combined breadcrumbs and remaining cheese. Bake for 20 minutes, or until the top is golden brown.

SERVES 4

flat

Fresh vegetable lasagne with arugula

Balsamic syrup
4 tablespoons balsamic vinegar
1½ tablespoons brown sugar

16 thin, fresh asparagus spears,
   trimmed and cut into 2-inch
   lengths
1 cup peas
2 large zucchini, cut into
   thin ribbons

2 fresh lasagne sheets
3 cups arugula
1 large handful basil, torn
2 tablespoons olive oil
1 cup ricotta cheese
5½ oz sun-dried tomatoes
shaved parmesan cheese,
   to serve

Stir the vinegar and brown sugar in a saucepan over medium heat until the sugar dissolves. Reduce the heat and simmer for 3–4 minutes. Remove from the heat.

Bring a saucepan of salted water to a boil. Blanch the asparagus, peas, and zucchini in separate batches until just tender. Remove with a slotted spoon and refresh each batch in cold water. Drain well. Return the cooking liquid to the boil. Cook the lasagne sheets in the water for 1–2 minutes, or until *al dente*. Drain. Cut each sheet in half lengthways.

Toss the vegetables and the arugula with the basil and olive oil. Season. Place one strip of pasta on a plate—one-third on the center of the plate and two-thirds overhanging one side. Place some salad on the center one-third, topped with some ricotta, and tomato. Season and fold over one-third of the lasagne sheet. Top with another layer of salad, ricotta, and tomato. Fold back the final layer of pasta and garnish with salad and tomato. Repeat with the remaining pasta, salad, ricotta and tomato. Drizzle with the balsamic syrup and serve with the parmesan.

SERVES 4

Roast squash
sauce on pappardelle

3 lbs 2 oz winter squash, such as butternut,
   cut into ¾-inch thick pieces
4 garlic cloves, crushed
3 teaspoons thyme, plus extra to serve
3½ fl oz olive oil
1 lb 2 oz pappardelle
2 tablespoons light whipping cream
¾ cup hot chicken stock
1 oz shaved parmesan cheese

Preheat the oven to 400°F. Combine the squash, garlic, thyme, and 3 tablespoons of the olive oil in a bowl and toss together. Season.

Transfer to a baking tray and cook for 30 minutes, or until tender and golden.

Meanwhile, cook the pasta in a large saucepan of boiling salted water until *al dente*. Drain well and return to the pan to keep warm. Toss through the remaining oil and keep warm.

Place the squash and the cream in a food processor or blender and process until smooth. Add the hot stock and process until smooth and combined. Season and gently toss through the pasta. Sprinkle with parmesan and extra thyme, if desired.

SERVES 4

Lasagnette with spicy chicken meatballs

1 lb 10 oz ground chicken
2 tablespoons chopped cilantro leaves,
   plus extra, to garnish
1½ tablespoons red curry paste
2 tablespoons oil
1 red onion, finely chopped
3 garlic cloves, crushed
3½ cups ready-made tomato pasta sauce
2 teaspoons brown sugar
12 oz lasagnette

Line a tray with baking paper. Combine the meat, cilantro, and 1 tablespoon of the curry paste. Roll heaped tablespoons of the mixture into balls and put on the tray. Refrigerate.

Heat the oil in a large deep frying pan over medium heat. Cook the onion and garlic for 2–3 minutes, or until softened. Add the remaining curry paste and cook, stirring, for 1 minute, or until fragrant. Add the pasta sauce and sugar and stir well. Reduce the heat and add the meatballs. Cook, turning halfway through, for 10 minutes, or until the meatballs are cooked through.

Meanwhile, cook the pasta in a large saucepan of boiling salted water until *al dente*. Drain well and return to the pan to keep warm.

Serve topped with the sauce and meatballs. Garnish with cilantro, if desired.

SERVES 4

Tuna and chermoula on pappardelle

2 small sweet potatoes, cut into ¾-inch cubes
3½ fl oz olive oil
1¼ cups finely chopped cilantro leaves
1⅓ cups chopped Italian parsley
3 garlic cloves, crushed
3 teaspoons ground cumin
3 tablespoons lemon juice
4 x 6 oz tuna steaks
14 oz pappardelle

Preheat the oven to 400°F. Toss the sweet potato in 2 tablespoons of the oil. Place on a baking tray and roast for 25–30 minutes, or until tender.

To make the chermoula, put the cilantro, parsley, garlic, cumin, and ¾ teaspoon cracked black pepper in a small food processor and process until a rough paste forms. Transfer to a bowl and stir in the lemon juice and 1 tablespoon of the oil.

Put the tuna in a non-metallic bowl, cover with 2 tablespoons of the chermoula and toss. Marinate in the refrigerator for 20 minutes.

Meanwhile, cook the pasta in a large saucepan of boiling salted water until *al dente*. Drain well and return to the pan to keep warm. Mix in the remaining chermoula and oil.

Heat a lightly oiled chargrill pan or barbecue hotplate over high heat. Cook the tuna for 2 minutes on each side, or until done to your liking. Cut into ¾-inch cubes and toss through the pasta with the sweet potato.

SERVES 4

Stracci with artichokes and chargrilled chicken

1 tablespoon olive oil

3 boneless, skinless chicken breasts

1 lb 2 oz stracci

8 slices prosciutto

10 oz jar artichokes in oil, drained and chopped, oil reserved

1 cup thinly sliced sun-dried tomatoes,

2¾ oz baby arugula

2–3 tablespoons balsamic vinegar

Lightly brush a frying or chargrill pan with the oil and heat over high heat. Cook the chicken for 6–8 minutes each side, or until cooked through. Cut into thin slices on the diagonal.

Meanwhile, cook the pasta in a large saucepan of boiling salted water until *al dente*. Drain well and return to the pan to keep warm.

Put the prosciutto on a lined baking tray and cook under a hot broiler for 2 minutes each side, or until crisp. Cool slightly and break into pieces.

In a bowl, combine the pasta with the chicken, prosciutto, artichokes, tomato, and arugula and toss. Whisk together 3 tablespoons of the reserved artichoke oil and the balsamic vinegar and toss through the pasta mixture. Season.

SERVES 6

Freeform ricotta and mushroom lasagne

1 cup ricotta cheese
2/3 cup grated parmesan cheese
3½ tablespoons olive oil
1 onion, thinly sliced
2 garlic cloves, crushed
1 lb 2 oz brown mushrooms, sliced
10½ fl oz ready-made tomato pasta sauce
6 sheets fresh lasagne, cut in half, then cut into
    4½-inch squares
4 cups baby spinach leaves, washed

Mix the ricotta with half the parmesan and season. Heat 2 tablespoons of the oil in a large frying pan, add the onion and cook for 2 minutes, or until it softens. Add the garlic and mushrooms and cook for 1–2 minutes, or until the mushrooms start to soften. Add the tomato pasta sauce and cook for a further 5–6 minutes, or until the sauce starts to thicken. Season well.

Meanwhile, cook the pasta in a large saucepan of boiling salted water until *al dente*. Drain well and return to the pan to keep warm.

Put the spinach in a pan with just a little water clinging to the leaves. Cover and cook over medium heat for 1–2 minutes, or until the spinach has wilted.

To assemble, place a pasta square on the base of each plate. Top with the mushroom sauce, then place another pasta square on top. Spread the ricotta mixture evenly over the surface, leaving a 3/4-inch border. Top with the spinach. Place another pasta square on top, drizzle with oil, then sprinkle with the parmesan. Season.

SERVES 4

Creamy chicken and peppercorn pappardelle

2 boneless, skinless chicken breasts
1 oz butter
1 onion, halved and thinly sliced
2 tablespoons drained green peppercorns, slightly crushed
½ cup white wine
10½ fl oz light whipping cream
14 oz fresh pappardelle
4 tablespoons sour cream (optional)
2 tablespoons chopped chives

Cut the chicken in half so that you have four flat fillets and season. Melt the butter in a frying pan over medium heat. Add the chicken and cook for 3 minutes on each side, or until lightly browned and cooked through. Remove from the pan, cut into slices and keep warm.

Add the onion and peppercorns to the same pan and cook over medium heat for 3 minutes, or until the onion has softened slightly. Add the wine and cook for 1 minute, or until reduced by half. Stir in the cream and cook for 4–5 minutes, or until thickened slightly, then season.

Meanwhile, cook the pasta in a large saucepan of boiling salted water until *al dente*. Drain well and return to the pan to keep warm.

Mix together the pasta, chicken and any juices, and cream sauce. Serve topped with sour cream and sprinkled with chives.

SERVES 4

Blue cheese and
walnut lasagnette

13 oz lasagnette
1 cup walnuts
1½ oz butter
3 French shallots, finely chopped
1 tablespoon brandy or cognac
1 cup crème fraîche
7 oz gorgonzola cheese, crumbled (see Note)
1⅓ cups baby spinach leaves

Preheat the oven to 400°F. Cook the pasta in a large saucepan of boiling salted water until *al dente*. Drain well and return to the pan to keep warm.

Meanwhile, put the walnuts on a baking tray and roast for 5 minutes, or until golden and toasted. Cool, then roughly chop.

Heat the butter in a large saucepan over medium heat. Add the shallots and cook for 1–2 minutes, or until soft. Add the brandy and simmer for 1 minute, then stir in the crème fraîche and gorgonzola. Cook for 3–4 minutes, or until the cheese has melted and the sauce has thickened.

Stir in the spinach and toasted walnuts, reserving 1 tablespoon for garnish. Heat gently until the spinach has just wilted. Season. Gently mix the sauce through the pasta. Serve sprinkled with the reserved walnuts.

SERVES 4

NOTE: The gorgonzola needs to be young as this gives a sweeter, milder flavour to the sauce.

Pappardelle with salmon and gremolata

½ cup chopped Italian parsley
3 teaspoons grated lemon zest
2 garlic cloves, finely chopped
14 oz pappardelle
3 tablespoons extra virgin olive oil
1 lb 2 oz fresh salmon fillet
2 teaspoons olive oil, extra

To make the gremolata, put the parsley, lemon zest, and garlic in a bowl and mix together well.

Cook the pasta in a large saucepan of boiling salted water until *al dente*. Drain well and return to the pan. Add the olive oil and toss gently. Add the gremolata to the pan with the pasta and toss.

Remove the skin and any bones from the salmon. Heat the extra olive oil in a frying pan over medium heat. Cook the salmon for 3–4 minutes, turning once during cooking. Take care not to overcook the fish. Flake the salmon into large pieces and toss through the pasta. Season.

SERVES 4

Freeform wild mushroom lasagne

¼ oz dried porcini mushrooms
12 oz mixed wild mushrooms (such as shiitake, oyster, and brown)
1 oz butter
1 small onion, halved and thinly sliced
1 tablespoon chopped thyme
3 egg yolks
½ cup heavy whipping cream
1 cup grated parmesan cheese
8 fresh lasagne sheets (4 x 10 inch)

Soak the porcini in 3 tablespoons boiling water for 15 minutes. Strain through a sieve, reserving the liquid. Cut the larger mushrooms in half.

Heat the butter in a frying pan over medium heat. Cook the onion for 2 minutes, or until just soft. Add the thyme, mushrooms, and porcini and cook for about 1–2 minutes, or until softened. Add the reserved mushroom liquid and cook for 2 minutes, or until the liquid has evaporated. Set aside.

Beat the egg yolks, cream, and half the parmesan in a large bowl. Cook the pasta in a large saucepan of boiling salted water until *al dente*. Drain well and toss gently in the egg mixture. Reheat the mushrooms.

To serve, place one sheet of folded lasagne on a plate. Top with some mushrooms, then another sheet of folded lasagne. Drizzle with any remaining egg mixture and sprinkle with the remaining parmesan.

SERVES 4

Roast duck with fresh pappardelle

9 oz baby pak choy, washed and
   leaves separated
1 lb 5 oz fresh pappardelle
1 Chinese roast duck, skin removed (see Note)
4 tablespoons peanut oil
3 garlic cloves, crushed
3 teaspoons finely chopped fresh ginger
¾ cup chopped cilantro leaves
2 tablespoons hoisin sauce
2 tablespoons oyster sauce

Bring a large saucepan of water to a boil and blanch the pak choi for 1–2 minutes, or until tender, but still crisp. Remove with a slotted spoon and keep warm.

Meanwhile, cook the pasta in a large saucepan of boiling salted water until *al dente*. Drain well and return to the pan to keep warm.

Remove the duck meat from the bones and finely shred. Heat the peanut oil in a small saucepan over high heat and bring it up to smoking point. Remove from the heat and allow to cool for 1 minute, then swirl in the garlic and ginger to infuse the oil. Be careful not to allow the garlic to burn or it will turn bitter.

Pour the hot oil over the pasta and add the pak choi, duck, cilantro, hoisin, and oyster sauces. Toss well, season and serve immediately.

SERVES 4–6

NOTE: Chinese roast duck can be bought from Asian specialty shops.

Smoked salmon
stracci in Champagne sauce

13 oz fresh stracci (see Note)
1 tablespoon olive oil
2 large garlic cloves, crushed
½ cup Champagne
1 cup heavy whipping cream
7 oz smoked salmon, cut into thin strips
2 tablespoons small capers in brine, rinsed and squeezed dry
2 tablespoons chopped chives
2 tablespoons chopped dill

Cook the pasta in a large saucepan of boiling salted water until *al dente*. Drain well and return to the pan to keep warm.

Meanwhile, heat the oil in a large frying pan over medium heat. Cook the garlic for 30 seconds. Pour in the Champagne and cook for 2 minutes, or until the liquid is reduced slightly. Add the cream and cook for about 3–4 minutes, or until the sauce has thickened.

Add the sauce, salmon, capers, and herbs to the pasta and toss gently. Season.

SERVES 4

NOTE: Stracci is sold fresh and dried—either is suitable for this recipe—or you can use fresh or dried fettucine or tagliatelle.

Seafood lasagne

1 tablespoon olive oil

1 oz butter

1 onion, finely chopped

2 garlic cloves, crushed

14 oz shrimp, peeled and deveined

1 lb 2 oz firm white fish fillets, cut into small pieces

9 oz scallops with roe

1 lb 10 oz ready-made tomato pasta sauce

1 tablespoon concentrated tomato purée

1 teaspoon brown sugar

½ cup grated cheddar cheese

3 tablespoons grated parmesan cheese

9 oz lasagne sheets

Cheese sauce

4¼ oz butter

⅔ cup all-purpose flour

6 cups milk

2 cups grated cheddar cheese

1 cup grated parmesan cheese

Preheat the oven to 350°F. Grease a 10-cup ovenproof dish. Heat the oil and butter in a saucepan. Add the onion and cook for 2–3 minutes. Add the garlic and cook for 30 seconds. Add the shrimp and fish and cook for 2 minutes, then add the scallops. Cook for 1 minute. Stir in the tomato pasta sauce, tomato purée, and sugar and simmer for 5 minutes.

To make the sauce, melt the butter in a saucepan over low heat, then stir in the flour and cook for 1 minute. Stir in the milk. Simmer for 2 minutes, stirring, then mix in the cheddar and parmesan cheeses. Season.

Line the dish with a layer of lasagne sheets. Spoon one-third of the seafood sauce into the dish. Top with one-third of the cheese sauce. Repeat until you have three layers, ending with a layer of cheese sauce. Sprinkle with the cheeses. Bake for 30 minutes, or until golden.

SERVES 6

Pappardelle with lamb shank, rosemary, and red wine ragù

1½ tablespoons olive oil
1 large onion, finely chopped
1 large carrot, finely diced
2 celery stalks, finely diced
2 bay leaves
3 lbs 5 oz lamb shanks
4 garlic cloves, finely chopped
1 tablespoon chopped rosemary

3 cups dry red wine
4 cups beef stock
2 cups puréed tomatoes
½ teaspoon finely grated lemon zest
1 lb 2 oz pappardelle
Italian parsley leaves, to garnish

Heat 1 tablespoon of the oil in a large saucepan over medium heat. Add the onion, carrot, celery, and bay leaves and cook, stirring often, for 10 minutes, or until the onion is lightly browned. Remove from the pan.

Heat some extra oil in the pan and cook the lamb shanks in two batches, turning occasionally, for 15 minutes, or until browned. Remove from the pan. Add the garlic and rosemary to the pan. Cook for 30 seconds, or until golden.

Return the vegetables to the pan, then stir in the wine, stock, puréed tomatoes, zest, and 1 cup water. Add the shanks and bring to a boil. Reduce the heat and simmer, uncovered, for 2¼ hours, or until the lamb is tender.

Cook the pasta in a saucepan of boiling salted water until *al dente*. Drain well and return to the pan to keep warm. Remove the shanks from the sauce and remove the meat from the bones. Return the meat to the sauce and stir. Season. Toss the pasta through the sauce. Garnish with the parsley.

SERVES 6–8

Squash, spinach, and ricotta lasagne

3 tablespoons olive oil
3 lbs 5 oz winter squash, such as butternut,
   cut into ½-inch dice
1 lb 2 oz spinach leaves, trimmed
4 fresh lasagne sheets
2 cups ricotta cheese
2 tablespoons light whipping cream
3 tablespoons grated parmesan cheese
pinch ground nutmeg

Heat the oil in a non-stick frying pan over medium heat. Add the squash and cook, stirring occasionally, for 15 minutes, or until tender. Season and keep warm.

Cook the spinach in a large saucepan of boiling water for 30 seconds, or until wilted. Using a slotted spoon, transfer to a bowl of cold water. Drain well and squeeze out as much excess water as possible. Finely chop the spinach. Add the lasagne sheets to the saucepan of boiling water and cook, stirring occasionally, until *al dente*. Drain. Cut each sheet widthways into thirds.

Combine the ricotta, cream, parmesan, spinach, and nutmeg in a small saucepan over low heat. Stir for 2–3 minutes, or until warmed through.

Place a piece of lasagne on the base of each plate. Using half the squash, top each of the sheets, then cover with another piece of lasagne. Use half the ricotta mixture to spread over the lasagne sheets, then add another lasagne piece. Top with the remaining squash, then remaining ricotta mixture. Season well and serve immediately.

SERVES 4

Pappardelle with salami, leek, and provolone cheese

13 oz pappardelle
2 tablespoons olive oil
2 leeks, thinly sliced (including some of the green section)
2 tablespoons white wine
1 lb 12 oz canned diced tomatoes
5½ oz sliced mild salami, cut into strips
1 large handful basil leaves, torn
4½ oz provolone cheese, cut into
   1¼-inch thick strips
1 oz grated parmesan cheese

Cook the pasta in a large saucepan of boiling salted water until *al dente*. Drain well and return to the pan to keep warm.

Meanwhile, heat the olive oil in a large deep frying pan over low heat. Add the leek and cook for 4 minutes, or until soft but not browned. Increase the heat to medium, add the wine and stir until almost evaporated.

Add the tomato and salami. Season and simmer for 5 minutes, or until reduced slightly. Toss the tomato sauce mixture, basil, and provolone lightly through the pasta. Sprinkle with the parmesan.

SERVES 4

index

This 2008 edition published by Barnes & Noble, Inc.,
by arrangement with Murdoch Books Pty Limited.

Chief Executive: Juliet Rogers
Publishing Director: Kay Scarlett

Design manager: Vivien Valk
Series editor: Jane Price
Project manager: Gordana Trifunovic
Design concept: Alex Frampton
Designer: Susanne Geppert
Production: Nikla Martin
Introduction text: Leanne Kitchen
Recipes developed by the Murdoch Books Test Kitchen

Barnes & Noble, Inc.
122 Fifth Avenue
New York, NY 10011

ISBN-13: 978-1-4351-0825-7
ISBN-10: 1-4351-0825-6

10 9 8 7 6 5 4 3 2 1

Printed by Sing Cheong Printing Co. Ltd in 2008. PRINTED IN HONG KONG.

IMPORTANT: Those who might be at risk from the effects of salmonella poisoning
(the elderly, pregnant women, young children and those suffering from immune
deficiency diseases) should consult their doctor with any concerns about eating raw eggs.

OVEN GUIDE: You may find cooking times vary depending on the oven
you are using. For fan-forced ovens, as a general rule, set the oven temperature to
35°F lower than indicated in the recipe.